POWER
Play

POWER *Play*

Breaking through bias, barriers and boys' clubs

Julia **BANKS**

Hardie Grant
BOOKS

Published in 2021 by Hardie Grant Books, an imprint of Hardie Grant Publishing

Hardie Grant Books (Melbourne)
Wurundjeri Country
Building 1, 658 Church Street
Richmond, Victoria 3121

Hardie Grant Books (London)
5th & 6th Floors
52–54 Southwark Street
London SE1 1UN

hardiegrantbooks.com

A catalogue record for this book is available from the National Library of Australia

Power Play
ISBN 978 1 74379 720 4

10 9 8 7 6 5 4 3 2 1

Cover design by Alissa Dinallo
Typeset in 12.5/17 pt Adobe Garamond by Post Pre-press Group
Printed in Australia by Griffin Press, part of Ovato, an Accredited ISO AS/NZS 14001 Environmental Management System printer.

The paper this book is printed on is certified against the Forest Stewardship Council® Standards. Griffin Press holds FSC® chain of custody certification SGSHK-COC-005088. FSC® promotes environmentally responsible, socially beneficial and economically viable management of the world's forests.

Hardie Grant acknowledges the Traditional Owners of the country on which we work, the Wurundjeri people of the Kulin nation and the Gadigal people of the Eora nation, and recognises their continuing connection to the land, waters and culture. We pay our respects to their Elders past, present and emerging

To my beloved mum – my first role model.

To my husband – my great life love;
and to our son and daughter – who fill
my heart with unconditional love.

Contents

'Often when good women call out or are subjected to bad behaviour, the reprisals, backlash and commentary portrays them as the bad ones: the liar, the troublemaker, the emotionally unstable or weak, or someone who should be silenced.'

Julia Banks, Australian House of Representatives, 27 November 2018

INTRODUCTION

'Who's going to look after your kids?' The question was put to me abruptly and unashamedly, the interviewer's tone aggressive. 'You'll be constantly travelling and away for work.'

I was taken aback, but I remained Zen-like as I replied. 'My kids have grown up with both their parents working. They're self-sufficient, older and ...'

'Exactly how old are they?' The interviewer impatiently interrupted. She fired her questions down the phone like bullets, demanding efficient replies.

Still somewhat Zen-like, I replied, 'In their late teens.'

'Good God, how old are you then?' she asked.

Zen switched to incredulity. *Am I really being asked this question?* But I answered, 'Fifty-two.'

'Well then, you're too old.' And with that, the conversation concluded.

I am sure this experience would not have been all that surprising to women who started in the workforce in the 1970s and 80s or even the 90s. During one of my first job interviews, as a young, newly qualified lawyer, the HR guy had said, 'Mmm, well, I'm not supposed to ask this question, but you *are* a young woman of childbearing age: how are you going to cope with a full-time job if you go off and have babies?' The introduction of the Sex Discrimination Act in 1984 had still been a 'work in progress' as far as that guy was concerned. Again, in the early 1990s, my nervous excitement had turned to disbelief when a bank manager said that 'his bank' (one of the big four) would only give us a loan based on my soon-to-be husband's income, not mine – because I would 'likely give up work and have children'.

But this conversation wasn't taking place in the 1980s or 90s. This was 2015. That year, when the newly installed prime minister of Canada, Justin Trudeau, was asked to explain his gender parity promise – of an equal number of men and women in his cabinet – he had said simply, 'Because it's 2015.'

Granted, this was a job interview with a difference: it was one among a series of phone conversations and coffee meetings to be completed by anyone contemplating or seeking preselection to be a candidate in a federal election for a major political party.

Like most women, I have many stories that pertain to gender inequality, but this one was a standout – not least because it was 2015. It was one of those exchanges you have that leaves you feeling rattled and uneasy. I got up from my desk, went outside to get some air and phoned a friend. 'You wouldn't believe the conversation I just had …' At times like these, the sisterhood is still what you draw on.

If you tick one or some of the boxes, discrimination, barriers, misogyny and bias come with the territory, and throughout my career I ticked most of the boxes at one time or another. Woman – tick. Young woman – tick. Forty-something woman – tick. Fifty-something woman – tick. Single woman – tick. Married woman – tick. Full-time worker and mother of two – tick. Woman of non-Anglo-Saxon heritage – tick. Older woman – tick.

None of this stopped me playing the game day after day.

I'm also short and small in stature, for which no high heel can compensate. 'Petite,' say my friends. 'Small but power-packed,' said a work colleague.

In a world where the other players were all men, my physical size and strength put me at a disadvantage in some forms of the game. The field of play: the boardroom. The opening tactic: the handshake.

I once found myself surreptitiously stretching my hand backwards and forwards thinking, *God that hurt.* Play continued, with everyone taking their strategic positions around the enormous boardroom table. Every other person was an older, white male, except for one younger man – who had compensated by ramping up his handshake methodology from 'firm' to ridiculous. (One of my older male colleagues confirmed the strategy as 'just a power thing' – that younger handshake assaulter was hoping to subliminally assert himself a little more.) No doubt most, if not all, of the men sitting around that table had similar lived experiences, which meant similar values, tactics and skills were the name of this game. They all intuitively understood the same power plays – from the opening handshake to the negotiation styles that were played across the table.

Throughout my career I have always worked in blokey cultures. The makeup of people around these boardroom tables is slowly changing – but 'slowly' is the operative word. 'Not fast enough' is the reality. The business case has been made time and again that diversity delivers success in terms of profit and workplace culture, and yet all too often it feels like this information is falling on deaf ears.

I don't believe that effective leadership traits are gendered. Rather, good traits are weighted differently based on different lived experiences. Throughout history, many older white males have been great leaders, led successful businesses and governments, and empowered future successful leaders. Many I have worked with. The best leaders have encompassed compassion and empathy in their style, be that for their employees, their stakeholders, their citizens or their customers. But lived experiences of people of different genders, different ages, different cultural backgrounds, sexualities and abilities all shape leadership styles and create different voices – all of which need to be seen and heard if we are to make a world where all people are represented and treated equally.

Still, it remains as true today as it did years ago that cultural prejudice, ageism and sexism all lurk, overlap and intersect in the corridors of power and in all workplace cultures. Sometimes, these forces remain unseen – covered up or hidden in unconscious parts of the mind – only surfacing from time to time in unexamined speech or action. Other times they are part of a pattern, occurring so regularly that they might feel mundane and innocuous. Either way, these forces create roadblocks that thwart people's leadership journeys.

Our society – be it parliament or workplace, the school playground or the sporting arena – is structured on power. Power in all its glorious and inglorious forms. Power for good and for bad. Power used to make a difference and power used to keep things the same. The power of financial and personal independence and the power of silence or being silenced. Unspoken, historical and structural rules around power. Power used to amplify the voices of others. The possibilities when power intersects with courage and the gift of time.

Positions of power aren't confined to the office held, the title or to politics. Power doesn't just manifest itself in overtly powerful positions, and it's not limited to institutional power. It includes the power of the team as much as it does the personal power of the individual. Power in all its forms is everywhere in the workplace. It is in the public and private sector in equal measure. It is in the corporate sector, the legal and medical professions, and in academia. It is in local councils and small to medium business. It is in sport, the arts and the media.

But the fact is, there are more men than women holding this power. Men have more power over our society, our economy, and our future.

Sometimes the family structure you grow up in can be your first experience of bias and barriers. But it's often when people start work, even in a casual after-school job, that they discover these biased forces at play. Entering the workplace is metaphorically and physically like entering a new building. It's a new structure. And within it there are hierarchies. There are the more senior players, the more experienced players, the good players, the bad players, the weak and the strong, the coaches, the support staff, the cheats, the bullies and the mentors. They're all there. Entering this workplace structure often coincides with a time when people are harnessing or establishing their own sense of self and purpose – and figuring out what's important to them. They may incorporate these existing structures of power into their own self-image and learn how to work within them. Or they may choose to resist them, try to change them or walk away from them.

Gender equality has always been important to me, for as far back as I can remember. I've always believed that men and women should have equal political, social and economic rights, and championed individual women in the workplace. During the twenty-plus years of my legal and corporate career, I saw first-hand a slow metamorphosis of the workplace culture towards gender equality. The private legal sector was way behind the corporate world on this front, though I think it's pretty well documented that most sectors have 'issues' – some more than others. Because I worked for corporate organisations whose hearts were in the right place, the more senior I became the more I found that I had the space and voice where my advocacy could help others, in big ways and small. My advocacy for gender equality has been consistently integrated into my 'day job' – sometimes without my realising it.

The experiences I had as I climbed through the ranks towards leadership positions had their ups and downs. The ups included the people I encountered (many of whom became dear friends), the achievements, the challenges met, the travel, the excitement that came with each promotion and the personal satisfaction from my corporate career. Not all the downs were related to the barriers, bias and discrimination, but many were.

By the late 1990s things were starting to improve, and so I surprised myself with what I said to my baby daughter just hours after she was born. It was our first mother–daughter connection. I whispered to her peaceful cherubic face that I would do everything I could in my life to make the world a better place for her – a place where she could have equal opportunities to those of her older brother.

I'd never thought this or planned to say it to her – it came from a very visceral maternal place. At the time I sincerely believed that with the passing of, say, a decade we would be there. Two decades have passed. We're not there yet.

*

In my many and varying roles throughout my career, both in a formal and informal capacity, I've fielded questions from girls and women of all ages about their career aspirations: from leading executive training sessions, to mentoring women navigating the 'mummy wars' and juggling full-time work, to speaking with groups of young senior students, to being on a panel in a packed Sydney Opera House on International Women's Day. These questions have most often been centred around how to reach a leadership position – about 'how it all works on the inside', and how to get there. How to navigate around bias and barriers, or storm through them.

Many so-called answers to these questions have found form in conferences, books, podcasts, workshops, forums and networking events, and many are based on the premise that there is something women need to do more of, be more of or fix about themselves. The truth is, there's nothing wrong with women. But there's a lot wrong with the current power structures.

Millions of women have got through the cut and thrust to reach these positions of power, and millions are in the pipeline. But we still hear 'we can't find the women' in response to calls for gender-equal leadership teams. The corporate world still has some work to do. The world of federal politics has a lot more to do.

After a long and steady career in the private sector, I lived and breathed a short but intense period in politics. Just as I entered my business career with no business connections or insider knowledge in my twenties, I entered the world of federal politics with no political connections or insider knowledge in my fifties. They were calling for 'more women', and so I joined up. I'd experienced and knew that having a leadership position gives power to your voice and gives you influence. This was an opportunity to have my voice heard on a broader platform in advocacy on important community and societal issues, such as education and health, climate change action and gender and cultural equality.

Entering politics was like entering another world. It was a world stuck in time, and so deficient in areas of trust and rational judgement that it would at times be astounding to even the most seasoned corporate-business-trained outsider. I felt like I was an extra in a nightmare TV series, a hybrid between *Mad Men* and *House of Cards*. The 'who is going to look after your children' interview was not a quirky, one-off aberration. It was the tip of a very big iceberg of brutal and overt conscious bias – as opposed to the more polite unconscious variety I'd experienced in my corporate career. It became clear that the call for 'more women' was more about keeping up with political opponents (who had introduced a quota system in the mid-1990s) and securing 'the women's vote', and less about recognising that this was more than a numbers game.

Just over one year after I signed up, I was elected to the federal parliament as a government MP. It was the only seat won from the opposition, who had held it for eighteen years. I was lauded as winning 'the one seat in the one-seat majority'. 'You won us government' said a senior minister. I didn't feel suddenly powerful. Rather, I felt a mix of excitement, trepidation and determination. Excitement because of the sheer enormity of the historical moment. Trepidation because I sensed that after what I'd experienced since I put my hand up for preselection and in the lead up to the election win, there'd be worse to come. Determination because I knew that, no matter what, I was up to it.

I joined the Liberal Party in 2015 and was elected the following year. I served as a Liberal federal government MP under Malcolm Turnbull's prime ministership until the 2018 leadership coup that saw Scott Morrison become prime minister. Directly after that, I announced that I would not be recontesting my seat. Three months later, I quit the Liberal Party and completed my term of approximately six months in parliament as an independent MP. I then ran unsuccessfully as an independent candidate at the 2019 election.

Even though, at just over four years total, my time in politics was short compared to the spans in the rest of my career, in that period of time I got an insider's perspective on the most powerful forces in the country. At the same time, I acquired a public profile that exposed me not only to the disproportionate abuse and negativity that comes with the territory for women with a public profile, but also, and more importantly, to the thoughts, opinions and commentary of more outsiders than I could ever imagine. During this period, I experienced highly charged and condensed versions of sexism, power plays, bias and barriers to an extent that I didn't anticipate – even after everything I had already experienced in my career.

Following the 2018 leadership change, the irony was that the entrenched anti-women workplace culture became even more entrenched. The more transparent I was about the toxic workplace culture, the more the power exerted over me became gendered. The more vocal and transparent I was about issues, particularly gender equality, quotas, humanitarian issues and climate change action, the more the powerful forces played against me – and with such rat cunning, pervasive, Machiavellian tactics that there were times when I only realised and processed what they were doing long after they did it.

It was turbulent, and at times traumatic, but what got me through it were the equally powerful forces supporting me. I was filled with a sense of personal power by my loved ones, friends, old and new work colleagues, acquaintances and the general public across Australia

Being so publicly transparent during this time opened the floodgates of communication: commentary in the media, social media, emails, phone calls and direct messages. When I mentally carved out all of the negative messages, the remaining communication included people from of all walks of life, mainly women, who not only gave their support but also shared their own experiences. These messages gave me a crystal-clear picture of what is wrong, what needs fixing and what can and must be changed structurally across all workplaces, no matter the business or industry sector.

It was this that drove my decision to become an independent MP and to later run as an independent candidate. The commentariat and powers that be bizarrely painted it as 'revenge' for the coup – an act on behalf of the former prime minister. The gender games played on. In fact, I felt it was the only path I could take. I had unfinished business and wanted to use whatever personal power I had to continue to make a difference – particularly for gender equality. For our society, our economy and for future generations, we need an equal number of men and women to make the decisions that affect us all.

When I resigned from the Liberal Party, I was allotted 'no more than five minutes' by the parliamentary clerk for my 'statement on indulgence' (my resignation speech). That five-minute speech was not just about what I was experiencing at the time. It was underpinned by so many stories of barriers, bias and prejudice – both my firsthand accounts and those from others across the workplace spectrum.

Throughout my career, I've been the beneficiary of mentors, great leaders, advisors and numerous books. This book is written through my lens and with my stories, and through the stories of others. These stories explore how power and leadership go hand in hand, how to challenge powerful forces and, most importantly, how to use the power within yourself, not just for yourself but for others, throughout your leadership journey.

This book came about because I had a front row seat as an insider both in my legal corporate and in my political career. I've written it as an insider who's now out – without many of those constraints imposed by an employer, prospective employer, future lobbyist, political party or organisation. Even during my political career, I felt somewhat unshackled to speak my truth, especially compared to the career politicians who had 'grown up' in politics and carried the weight of historical quid pro quos. But I am not fearless. I will admit that, like so many women, I fear that in some cases going 'public' or 'on the record' with details and 'naming names' of those in power can potentially create an intolerable burden, threat or risk to one's emotional and financial wellbeing. This is particularly the case in stories that involve workplace misconduct, such as sexual harassment. For this reason, as well as for professional reasons, to maintain the privacy of other women and to show the pervasiveness of these issues, I have de-identified a lot of the stories.

This book isn't despairing about the many forms of barriers, bias and discrimination women encounter – nor is it a sanitised summary of them. Rather, it is about trusting in your inbuilt courage and using that power to take the next steps. It's about finding and always advocating for the structures and systems that will create equal workplace cultures. It's about both navigating towards leadership and navigating during leadership, whatever that might look like for you.

This is a book for the young student, the career woman of any age, the new mum returning to the workforce, the young parents organising child care in a rapidly changing world regarding caring responsibilities, or the older woman wanting a career change.

Whether you're anxious about your exam results, getting started, burning out, failing, succeeding, wondering 'what's next?' or 'is this it?' or living with some new curveball life has thrown you – I hope something in this book speaks to you.

I've tried to make this book as loud, clear and honest as it can be. No 'corporate speak', airbrushing, or telling you what you need to do 'more of' or 'be'. The aim is just to find your personal power to be yourself. To be part of that equal number in leadership. And to just be.

CHAPTER 1

That girl will go places

I looked out at the sea of young female faces, all senior students, in the school hall. Faces, hearts and minds that represented the multicultural diversity of Australia, full of hope and curiosity.

Like many times before, I'd been asked to do a speech about my career and achievements to a large group of students. I always made these speeches interactive, with the aim of making it more about the students than me. Throughout my career, I never received more rewarding feedback than when someone told me that I'd inspired them to aspire from one of these speeches. They were among my favourite moments.

After I was introduced and had made my way to the podium, I started my speech with a question. This always guaranteed attention with a young audience. I started with a question they would have been asked many times in their life, almost from the time they could string a sentence together, and probably more and more often towards the end of their school years.

'How many of you have been asked "What do you want to be when you grow up?"'

Almost all their hands went up.

'And how many of you have been asked "What are you going to do when you finish school?"'

Most hands stayed up.

'How many of you really know the answer to that question?'

A number of hands went down. Some tentatively. Some firmly and resolutely.

'How many of you have been told by someone or read somewhere to "dream big" and that "you can be whatever you want to be"?'

Hands were going up and down all over the room.

By now, these students were at an age where they would have realised there was a difference between wishful thinking and ambition. This cascade of hands reflected the diversity of their dreams and aspirations – and perhaps a difference in their backgrounds and experiences. Some of them might be suspicious of the glib advice to 'dream big'. Some might find it inspiring. Some might never have received that advice.

Sometimes when I was being introduced at one of these speeches, I would hear the oft-used phrase 'You can't be what you can't see'. I would always pause to think, *But there are millions of women around the world who have proven, throughout history, that they could be what they couldn't see.* When it comes to gender equality, or any other kind of diversity, there have always been women, throughout generations and up to the current day, who have pursued and become what they couldn't see. The suffragettes could clearly see what they couldn't yet be: voting women. From our first female prime minister, to the first Indigenous Australian to win an Olympic gold medal, to the first female

CEO of an ASX-listed company – all these women 'couldn't see' someone who looked like them, but they could see another path for themselves, and they had the opportunity to follow it.

The phrase is often quoted when congratulating a female world leader, a sporting hero, celebrity, or top executive in a male field, and it is meant to suggest that now other women can follow in that woman's path. But the more powerful form of inspiration that these leaders in their field can offer is not so much to suggest to other women that they should also be the next PM or Olympic gold medallist, but more that they can tailor and follow their own unique path. Young girls and women should be motivated to pursue an opportunity they hadn't anticipated, to aspire to what may seem insurmountable, to take a risk, to switch direction, to advocate for change, to be the change.

The excitement around the globe was palpable when Kamala Harris was elected as the first female vice president of the US. In her victory speech, she said, 'While I may be the first woman in this office, I will not be the last.' But while not every girl or woman who was celebrating the success of Harris would aspire to being the future US VP, in seeing Harris achieve this remarkable 'first' they would know that their own unique aspirations and visions for the future are possible.

As I looked out into the sea of faces, I could see that all of these young students, this next generation of women, had their own ambitions and their own visions. Many of them could have careers and jobs that haven't even been thought of yet in this changing world. Many of them could be 'firsts' in the field. My hope was that they would be given the opportunities to follow their ambitions – and the tools to surmount the obstacles.

*

At its most basic, the definition of ambition is 'a drive and determination to succeed'. But it's a vexatious word.

He's ambitious. She's ambitious.

One adjective. Two different meanings. Not according to the dictionary, but according to societal norms and expectations. For men it's usually a positive descriptor. For women, its usually a negative.

In doing research for a paper 'Do Women Lack Ambition?', Anna Fels noted that the women she interviewed 'hated the very word. For them, "ambition" necessarily implied egotism, selfishness, self-aggrandisement, or the manipulative use of others for one's own ends. None of them would admit to being ambitious.'

I've asked a number of women of all ages, all of whom are successful career women, what drives their ambition. I was surprised that some answered along the lines that they 'weren't really ambitious'. Most alluded to being independent. Many said things like, 'I want to always aim higher, to do the best I can do.' One of the most real answers I got was from a friend who has climbed the corporate ladder to the most senior position: 'Ultimately I really don't like being told what to do when I know I have the skills, experience and smarts to lead the great outcomes myself.'

In our glorious childhood phase, ambition is often unfettered, always unapologetic and generally very grand. Young boys and girls will declare that they want to be any number of things when they grow up, ranging from astronaut to rock star to prime minister. But through life, from a young age, ambition can go through different stages, can change and come and go. For women, it's often thwarted or suppressed, and for some women any sign of an outcome of ambition, such as a prestigious job title, nominals from a PhD or even a tertiary degree, can be a tool for mockery.

Ambition can look very different between different people, just as success manifests itself differently. We often have different drivers for what sets our ambition in motion, and depending on our experience, background and gender, we may have to fight harder than others to keep our ambition alive, and to pursue it.

I grew up in a different family environment to the one in which my children did. It was also very different to what was the traditional 1960 and 70s idyllic Brady-Bunch-style model – the one where the father is the traditional breadwinner and the mother is the homemaker. There was still lots of family love, a roof over our heads, food and happy times. But even though both my parents worked hard and long hours, there was always the dark thread of financial instability woven into our lives.

Through my childhood lens, I saw first-hand the effect of the constant presence of this thread and the conflict it created. It was always distressing. I knew my parents' arguments were usually about money and the lack of it.

I escaped and took solace in reading books and loved writing. My primary school down the road was my other comfort and constant. I loved the structure, the routine and the consistency school provided. *School will always be there, and so will books,* I would consciously tell my self. *Being able to learn will always be there.*

Both my parents had been denied an education for different reasons. My father was sent to Australia on his own as a fifteen-year-old boy to escape post-war poverty in Greece. His dreams of becoming a dentist were never to eventuate. Insecure and casual work waiting tables in restaurants and running his own small businesses were the source of his income for most of his life. My mother was born in Australia, but also of Greek heritage. She wanted to become a nurse, but her parents wouldn't support it or allow it, while her two brothers, one older and one younger, both became doctors.

Once, I was a witness to a lively disagreement between my parents – it was when my mother wanted to get her driver's licence but my dad disagreed. I remember thinking to my childhood self, *That's not fair.*

Around the same time, at what I now know was the peak period of their financial struggles and woes, they had another argument. Mum was desperate to take a full-time job to supplement their income, so she could 'make her own decisions' she said. My uncle, her brother, needed a receptionist at his medical clinic. My father didn't want her to take this job. Among other things, being a traditionalist, he thought it would be shameful for my mother to work full-time, as people would assume it meant that he couldn't support us.

My mother said she was just being pragmatic in taking this job. She had 'no choice'. Undoubtedly so. But she was also fighting for her freedom and independence. And mine. She was navigating through a culture that had defined her future in the context of a gender stereotype, and attempting to ensure a different future for me. Part of the reason Mum wanted the job was because I was approaching my high school years. Mum felt that the local public school 'wasn't good enough', as most girls who went to that school left well before Year 12, like she had. She wanted to earn money so she could send me to a local private school.

Mum eventually got her way and took the job. She also got her licence, and eventually replaced her bicycle with her own car. I went to the school that she chose – not an elite private school, a mid-tier one, but I was nevertheless acutely conscious of the financial pressure that it put on my parents. I remember feeling I'd failed, after being shortlisted for a scholarship but not winning it, and later coming across a bill for the school fees and feeling guilty. I was twelve.

I'm sure that's why my mum's tears were a backdrop for one of my first major learning experiences.

'Mummy, why are you crying?'

Mum was crouched over a table, sobbing. My childhood sense of anxiety and concern was deep and painful. She was finishing her work at home, counting dollar notes. These were 'the takings' of the day from my uncle's medical clinic – the brother who'd received the education she was denied.

The look of pain on her face, tears streaming down her cheeks, the sadness she seemed to be going through at that moment – I'll never forget. Just as I'll never forget the life lesson she taught me in her answer to this agonisingly vexed question from an innocent child.

'This –' she said, pointing to the wads of money in her hand – 'this is what an education will get you. *Never ever* depend on a man. *Never* be *controlled* by a man. Always be *independent.* Always have your own money.'

They were big words and thoughts for a young girl to hear. Packed with a raw emotion. But I took it all in. I remember the exact words and the exact scene, even though it happened nearly fifty years ago now. That exchange was the seed of my personal ambition.

My maiden speech in parliament made my mum cry, as did the ninety-second speech that I made in honour of her eightieth birthday (I presented her a framed Hansard copy of the speech as a gift): 'Mum's focus on ensuring that my brother and I had exactly the same opportunities, despite all the historical context in her life, has inspired my focus on gender and cultural equality and always helping those in need. Mum, you are the greatest role model, an inspiration and always will be.'

Throughout all my years of education, my sense of ambition never fit the glamourous 'dream big' or 'be whatever you want to be' format. I wanted financial security and independence. I had a very real sense that money would give me power over my own personal decision-making.

I wanted a job that was secure and paid me well. Getting a job I enjoyed and found interesting would be a 'bonus', not an essential – but I did feel excited about the possibility of a career in journalism or law. I loved the power of facts, the concept of parameters and the rule of law. I wanted to be the expert in the room. I also loved the power of true stories – reading or writing them.

A first roadblock, which I saw as a major setback, was my Year 12 results. After all the hard work, drive, determination and effort, I was two marks under the qualifying score to get into law at university. But my initial devastation changed to elation when the university offers came out; I had qualified to enter the law course on the provision that I maintained good grades in first year. I knew this was achievable but I really wanted to do everything I could to 'seal the deal'. I had this idea that getting some work experience in a law firm, which I would do for free, on top of getting good grades in first year, would secure my chances.

I nervously went to the law faculty office and stood in the reception area hoping to make an appointment to explore my idea with anyone in the department. But everyone was at lunch.

I was about to leave when a gentleman peered out of his office and said abruptly, 'Is someone there?' I thought this was a strange question given he was looking right in my direction. 'Who are you?' he said.

Feeling like an intruder, I gave him my name and explained my situation and my plan. The chasm between us grew suddenly smaller, not just because he walked over to be closer to me, but because he spoke more warmly and encouragingly.

He said, 'Don't do work experience for nothing! Those firms will exploit you. I know you'll be fine. You'll get over this provisional thing. You'll be a lawyer. And a good one. I know you will.'

'How?' I asked thinking he had some secret knowledge about the provisional grading system.

'I can tell. You've got that inner–' he stopped as if he couldn't articulate it, and then he put his arm to his heart. 'That inner drive. That ambition. It's in your heart.'

I found out later that this man was one of the heads of the law faculty. He was also totally blind. He couldn't see me, but he saw what was in my heart.

That short interaction taught me to pause and take stock of my self-worth. Of course, volunteering or true pro bono work can be deeply rewarding. When, a little later, I worked in the free legal service as a young student, I benefitted enormously from what that work taught me about humanity, even more than from what it taught me about law. But working for free shouldn't be an expected side-effect of ambition. Education, however, is a critical part of it.

I have enduring gratitude for being the beneficiary of free tertiary education. Not everyone is born into equal circumstances, and access to university, or at least affordable education, is a linchpin for gender equality. The importance of investment in education is often not regarded as highly as it should be – which I believe is why we don't pay our teachers enough in this country.

I never took my education for granted. At university, studying hard always took priority for me over parties and the pub, and in my spare time I took on casual work to support my tertiary life. I knew that, compared to most in my cohort, I had less 'fun' than they did. But I didn't feel unhappy or as if I were missing out. Rather, I was so genuinely grateful for the opportunity and didn't want to stuff it up.

But my unwavering and profound belief in the transformative powers of education meant that I naively thought that my degree would open doors as soon as I graduated. I was wrong.

All my law friends, almost without exception, had family or powerful connections within all the big and medium-sized law firms of note. An unspoken but widely known rule that still applies today is 'It's who you know'.

Without any connections of my own, I borrowed my aunt's typewriter and typed one hundred application letters to law firms across Melbourne. I typed them with confidence that I deserved this job based on all my hard work and academic achievement. Some answered, politely declining, but most didn't give me the courtesy of a response. I needed contingency plans, so I was also looking in the local paper classifieds for more casual work in case I didn't get a law job. Then a few of the letters scored me an interview. And from one of these coupled with a faint connection (a family friend had to see a lawyer after a car accident and mentioned my name), finally, I got my first job. I was thrilled.

But during the few years that followed, working in two different law firms in private practice, I slowly realised – with vague disbelief and a lot of denial – that I didn't want to be what I could see: the partners or even senior associates in their smart offices. Fundamentally, I didn't like being with just lawyers all day. I didn't like that files dealing with people's misery – divorce, child custody disputes and wills – areas of law which were traditionally given to women, were the only types of files that were being given to me.

I wanted commercial work with its different challenges: the

cut and thrust of commercial deals, litigation, contracts. Being the expert in the room while working with teams of people of all disciplines and skills. But that work seemed to be going to 'the boys'. It was only by chance, when a senior associate became ill during a big Federal Court commercial case, followed by his assistant junior lawyer having to go on unexpected personal leave, that a partner asked me to step in. The case went for a long time, and it was decided by the client and the partners that I would stay on it.

That 'step in' was my first step on my way out of private practice. I now had commercial experience on my CV, which made me of interest to a potential corporate recruiter wanting a junior in-house lawyer with commercial experience. Going into the commercial sector would guarantee me commercial work. And so, I set my sights on corporate law.

But it was seen as a step down in those days.

'So, you're joining the grubby world of commerce,' said one partner after I resigned to take on my first corporate role. 'I suppose you'll have a company cafeteria,' he sneered, making reference to the fact that my new corporate office wasn't in the legal precinct of the CBD (cue eye roll). He had a look on his face that screamed that I was a loser, but behind my polite smile my thought bubble said otherwise: I was nervous but excited about this change.

*

What drives ambition is personal. It can be based on a yearning for academic recognition, celebrity recognition, sporting success. It can come from admiring the dignity of work and knowing the value of money. It can be because of something a teacher said to you, or come from building on doing what you're good at. You may want to climb the career ladder, to be a leader in your field, to contribute to your community, to make a change. It can come from any life experience. I believe ambition often comes from people wanting to do the best job they can do, simply out of self-pride.

But many find that what keeps that sense of ambition alive long-term is a sense of purpose in striving to make a difference to someone else, directly or indirectly. That can manifest in the consultant or advertising executive who loves creating business solutions or being part of the creative process, in the healthcare professional who loves helping people get better, in the teacher or university lecturer who knows they've instilled new knowledge, in the accountant or economist who can communicate complex financial information to people. The sales rep who loves closing the deal, the writer or journalist who's got the bug to tell stories in pursuit of the truth, and the senior executive or CEO who loves making decisions that are going to help the people that work for them will all have an ambition sustained by the feeling of making a difference.

Aside from the certainty of financial independence, my career gave me that sense of purpose that comes with achieving something for others. Travelling to different places, meeting new people or mastering new skills were always a bonus, but not my real motivation. From the start, I loved coming up with solutions, defending clients, helping people in a crisis, implementing and training on governance procedures. I loved the collaboration, trust and mutual respect found in business. The sense of a common purpose and the proof that teamwork delivers success. I thrived on the rational thought and logic that is a prevailing feature of good businesses with good governance.

Once I moved into the corporate space, I also found opportunities came up that I had never even contemplated. That included an opportunity to work in a new sphere: corporate affairs. I became responsible for internal and external communications, media and crisis and risk management, and for leading and managing philanthropic programs. These jobs proved to be incredibly rewarding and challenging at the same time.

My corporate life wasn't always fabulous – it wasn't every day that I'd jump out of bed in the morning and be ready to start the day with verve and vigour. Of course, there were bad times – the worst being when you had to have the tough conversations or let go of good people because of budget cuts. There were bad bosses, poor-performing employees, people who abused your trust, failures, and moments when I'd have rather been somewhere else. There were many times when I reached the pinnacle of my corporate career and thought, *Is this it?* And there were many times when the sheer fatigue and busyness of work and life was so overwhelming, I wanted to just stay home and close the door, particularly when my husband and I were working full-time and raising two children.

But despite these lows, what got me out of bed in the morning was my sense of purpose: to do the best job I could do, and a job I could be proud of no matter the circumstances.

Being promoted can be an extrinsic motivation. As are rewards, recognition and accolades. They are, in a sense, badges of power. But what gives you real power is the people you work with – not just those who appoint you to these positions, but your peers and those who follow you, and especially those who respect and admire your leadership. It's that respect that underpins the power of the teams you lead.

As I was promoted to more senior leadership positions where I managed people and became responsible for making decisions that would directly affect the success of others and the success of the business, my job became increasingly challenging but increasingly rewarding – and both the challenges and the rewards increased my sense of purpose. What people saw and made of these promotions, though, was that I was ambitious. Which is usually fine for men … but gender stereotypes make it less fine for women.

As Mona Eltahawy puts it in her book *The Seven Necessary Sins for Women and Girls*, 'We learn early. "Bossy." "Bitch." "Show-off." "Selfish." "Pushy." The list of epithets that serve as synonyms for women who are perceived to be ambitious is a reminder of that sin of ambition.' I know several women, myself included, who've had the milder forms of those descriptions said about them in performance reviews: 'too outspoken', 'too strong-minded', 'too direct' or even just simply 'very ambitious' – like it's a bad thing.

In the world of business, I don't know how many times I've heard it said by senior and otherwise sensible people. They try to articulate what they don't like about a certain female leader, and they'll default to 'she's very ambitious'. It's either that or 'there's something about her I just don't like' – a comment so ubiquitous during the 2016 US election that Hillary Clinton's team created an acronym (TSAHIJDL) because they heard it so often.

The First Lady of the United States, Dr Jill Biden, has a bachelor's degree, two master's degrees and a doctor of education and announced she was keeping her teaching job because 'That's what I do'. Yet she was criticised for using her title because she's not a medical doctor. It wasn't a linguistic debate, rather a societal and sexist one. Closer to home, renowned writer Dr Julia Baird has borne the wrath of the social media sphere when using her title.

The higher her public profile or more successful a woman becomes, the more her voice is heard. A dark consequence is that the targeted gendered abuse becomes viler. Mary Beard, Britain's best-known classicist and a vocal feminist, has gone through the history of how powerful women have been treated from classical to modern times and demonstrates 'embedded ... mechanisms that silence women, that refuse to take them seriously and that sever them from the centres of power'.

This success–attack correlation seems to be particularly pronounced in politics.

From the time when I first announced I was running in the election, and then at every stage of my time in politics, my being ambitious or successful (interchangeable terms when you're a woman) was always used as a negative by my opponents – both within and outside the party.

If a woman with a public profile – who's therefore ostensibly seen as successful – makes a mistake, attacks on her are amplified far more than they would be if made on a man. Likewise, although ambition and success are intrinsically linked to personal wealth in the minds of many, that counts double when a woman is involved.

I experienced this first-hand when I made a mistake on a radio program. In the pressure of the moment, being conscious of the 'party line' and trying to stick to the message points, the words came out wrong, and after the interview it was promoted that I believed I could 'live on $40 a day'. Of course I don't believe that people could live on that. I was thinking of my parents' financial struggles. I was thinking in the context of people who had a roof over their heads thanks to the generosity of a family member or friend. I tried desperately to correct the record, but the siege of vitriol and abuse drowned this out. The attacks then ramped up to an acute level after an article was published outlining my current financial status (which was also compulsorily declared because of my MP status). Eventually, some months later, I got the opportunity to correct the record on the same program where it had all started, but even after that, on the campaign trail or occasionally on social media someone would call me a 'rich bitch'.

In this way, and in many other ways, people will try to break your ambition, to devalue your success or to diminish your reputation. The fact is, making a bold and ambitious career move or change requires courage. I believe everyone has the power of that courage deep in their heart. That's why the word courage comes from the Latin word meaning 'heart'.

My ambition had been a problem in politics from the start. When I drafted my first introductory brochure, I stated that I was a businesswoman and a corporate lawyer. A particularly misogynistic party elder baulked at what he saw as an act of rebellion: 'Take out all that bullshit career stuff. It might look good on your CV for your corporate mates, but will make you look like you're up yourself ... bloody ambitious.' How could I not put my career journey – an integral and defining part of the person I am and how I'd spent my entire adult life – on the information brochure headed 'About Julia'?

My experience of leaving my first legal job had some parallels to when I decided to run as an independent candidate in politics. One MP actually said to me, 'You'll never get another job.' An executive recruiter said, 'You'll never get offered a board position because boards don't like *single-issue* women.' They were both wrong. On election night an employee from the party I left sent me a drunken text message saying, 'Ha ha no greater pleasure than to see you crash and burn tonight'. He was also one of the many who had fed the whispering campaign that, because I was a former successful corporate executive, it followed that I was an 'ambitious rich bitch'.

As I learnt from my mum all that time ago, the partner to ambition is often financial independence. Throughout history and continuing to this day, many women don't have financial independence, often because it is out of their control or unattainable due to their life circumstances. And without financial independence women lack power.

Women not having financial parity to men is deeply intertwined with gender inequality and domestic violence. During my time as an MP, I supported women's refuges and understood that women's fears for their personal safety are often intertwined with their lack of financial security. This also drove my advocacy to retain the free legal services needed by women in domestic violence situations.

A reduced financial status also means a reduced career trajectory and slows down the journey of women getting into positions of power. Financial insecurity impacts women's ability to take risks and jump into new opportunities. It puts a dampener on their ambition. Nothing breaks your dreams like the fear of being out of a job and not able to support yourself or your family.

My mother's generation, as individuals and as a group, navigated through a 'man's world'. While some would say it's not a man's world anymore, most say would say we've still got a way to go – though it's often not articulated exactly how, why and where we need to go.

In Australia, and in many other countries, the COVID-19 crisis further articulated it for us.

In all my years of governance and issues management, I've seen that nothing identifies gaps more loudly and brutally than a crisis. The pandemic revealed huge gaps, including in relation to the gender pay gap and access to child care. Thousands of women around the world have been disproportionately affected, having to quit their jobs, go part-time or take extended leave to homeschool their kids – and suffering from mental health issues in part as a result. Job losses affected more women than men – especially given more women are employed in casual, part-time and insecure work. Women's unpaid work increased, and there was an increase in domestic violence. There is a real and legitimate concern that we are going to go backwards with regard to women's workforce participation. What this all means is that even with all the ambition in the world, financial stability starkly trumps all.

*

Ambition will inevitably look different at different stages of your life. There might be times of high achievement, great reward, recognition, and good luck. But there may also be failures and setbacks. There may not be instant gratification and there will sometimes be bad luck. Whatever your ambition looks like, it's important to embrace it, and not let others define it for you. But do accept that your personal sense of ambition can change, be extinguished or ignited. And know that you can repurpose your sense of purpose.

Once I was shopping with my two toddlers in tow. It was one of those frantic, pre-Christmas shopping trips: supermarket, department store, chemist, toy shop, bookstore. As I handed my credit card over to the cashier for what seemed like the tenth time, my son said, 'Mummy can I get one of those plastic things?'

'I want one, too' chimed in my younger daughter.

'What plastic things?' I said, already frazzled, looking around the store (I was thinking they meant another toy that would end up in landfill).

'One of those' he said, pointing to my credit card. 'Then I can buy whatever we want.'

My maternal commitment to role-modelling about finance and education came pouring out of my mouth ready-made. 'Well, to get one of these, you have to finish school and get a job, and then make money. Then you can get one.' I added with emphasis,

'Then you can make your own decisions.'

I think my three-year-old daughter took that to heart. One night, soon after our shopping jaunt, my husband picked her up from preschool. They arrived home, and she walked purposefully ahead of him through the front door. She had a mission. She changed into her pyjamas, grabbed some food, and started eating it in bed – all within the time it took my husband to put down his briefcase and flick through the mail on the hallway table. When he realised, he said, 'Oh darling, no. What are you doing? You have to have your bath, and we have to make dinner and have dinner all together when Mummy gets home–'

She interrupted him and replied deadpan, 'I make my own decisions.'

I loved the story so much. I was so proud that my baby girl had so much pluck.

I shared it as my small-talk contribution during the morning coffee break partway through a meeting of senior executives the next day. One male responded with one of those judgement-loaded, gender-stereotyped comments: 'I wonder where she gets her strong-willed *attitude* from.'

In response, the only other woman in the room made my day. She rolled her eyes at him and announced to all the executives around the board table, 'That girl will go places.'

Chapter 2

Dressed for battle

Dresses, high-heeled shoes, make up, nail polish, jewellery, handbags. I've loved all things feminine from as far back as I can remember. Particularly earrings – anyone who knows me knows that there's only one thing that makes a regular appearance on my birthday or Christmas wish list. In my teenage years I devoured *Dolly* magazine, and ever since then I have unashamedly loved reading fashion magazines and watching shows like *What Not to Wear* and *Sex and the City*.

I once asked a work colleague, whose grades in her undergraduate science degree had given her the option of going into medicine or law, why she had chosen law. She replied that she loved clothes and didn't want a job that meant she'd have to wear scrubs all day. I'll never know if she was joking, but I knew I wasn't alone in enjoying dressing for work.

I love fashion, and buying the right outfit for the right occasion. And my work clothes help me to play the part in whatever job I'm doing.

From the moment I started my first real job in the legal profession, I loved dressing for the job – even though my salary remained in the low levels in my first few years. I developed a knack for finding good things on sale and at wholesalers. But I was soon to discover that if you're a woman, the way you dress is considered everyone's business, including your boss's.

One Monday I came into work feeling particularly excited. On the weekend I'd found a bargain dress at a clearance sale. It was tailored like a suit, very conservative, and a beautiful deep red colour. With my black shoes and briefcase, I felt pretty schmick. What was more, I was going to court that day to assist the barrister. It would be one of my first days in a courtroom.

Or so I thought.

'Where do you think you're going?' said the partner.

'Court?' I replied quizzically, concerned about his tone.

'Not wearing that red dress you're not,' he said matter-of-factly.

The dress code for court, he explained with a tone mixed with frustration and condescension, was 'of subdued colour'. This lesson in my sartorial negligence came from a man who often wore gaudy, brightly coloured ties himself. He was the same partner who, when asked by a client 'How come you've got so many pretty women here?' replied, 'They're like flowers. Colourful and pretty. They make the office look nice.'

Crushed and embarrassed, I didn't get to go to court that day.

Two other women-lawyer acquaintances in my cohort, one now a judge, another a senior corporate lawyer, were told in no uncertain terms that wearing a pants suit was absolutely unacceptable dress code.

A popular affirmation that has held me in good stead during my career is 'pick your battles'. This wasn't going to be one of them. Navy and black. Skirts and dresses. These became my wardrobe staples.

'What did he think ... you were going to inflame the passions of the judge?' said a lawyer friend when I told her the story. While this may not have been his thought process, it turned out some judges had their own ways of treating young women differently, regardless of what we wore.

A couple of years later, boring dress code firmly in place, I was working late one evening when my concentration was interrupted by a file being dumped on my desk by a partner.

'Do this court mention matter for me. It's a standard adjournment request. Our barro [barrister] can't do it and none of the others [people more senior than me] are available. Supreme Court. Tomorrow morning, first thing.'

That was the extent of my lesson in how to do your first court appearance – although he did add that if the appearance took longer than two minutes, I'd know I'd 'screwed it up'. This guy was a senior partner, but apparently not a great leader. I prepared for the appearance late into the night, with neurotic diligence and a level of attention to detail that really wasn't warranted.

The Supreme Court is daunting at the best of times, but when I entered the courtroom the next morning it was something else. My lack of sleep was compensated for by the adrenalin surging through me. I had no choice but to go with 'fight' in the fight-or-flight syndrome that engulfed me. The court was packed with barristers – around fifty of them. And as far as I could see and hear, they were all men. Their deep, loud voices ricocheted off the cold walls of the courtroom, competing for attention as they bantered with each other as if they were in a bar without the booze. A sea of black gowns and white wigs cast a dark shadow over my presence; I felt invisible and conspicuous at the same time.

The judge entered, and a respectful silence immediately blanketed the austere courtroom. The mention matters were dealt with efficiently one by one. I was watching intently so I could copy and not 'screw up'.

I've got this, I told myself.

My case matter was called. I went to the front of the court and started. And was stopped at the ten-second mark.

Me: 'If your Honour pleases, I appear for the plaintiff and–'

Judge: 'Mzzzz … what was your name, I'm sorry …?'

He was emphasising my marriage-neutral title. I've always baulked at the Mrs title. Why should I declare my marital status to the world? Some criticise me for taking my husband's name, arguing its anti-feminist, but a name is personal and I wanted to share his name and that of my children. For me, the perfect compromise was retaining the title Ms.

What followed from the judge was a whole series of questions, bellowed down from his intimidating bench height in a part-mocking, part-condescending tone. Every question was accompanied by the unnecessary emphasis on the title Ms, with an elongated Z sound.

Judge: 'I don't have Form 234, Mzzzz …'

Me: 'If your honour pleases, I submitted that in line with the rules this morning.'

Judge: '… Oh, here it is. But, Mzzzz, what about …'

And so it continued.

A two-minute job took fifteen minutes. With each minute I became increasingly aware of the background noise. The sniggering from my wigged and gowned audience got louder.

I've clearly screwed this up somehow, I thought.

As I walked down William Street and headed back to the office, I was crushed and visibly shaking. The old enemy of self-doubt was my sole companion. I braced myself to report to the partner who'd gifted me with this 'opportunity' about the extent of my failure.

I stood at the doorway of the partners office and was midway through blurting out the story of my bad performance. Multitasking and only half-interested, the partner looked up and interrupted with a knowing smirk. 'I think I know what happened. Judge X has a *reputation*.' He brusquely indicated that he didn't need to hear anymore, and I should leave his office.

Despite this comment, I put it all down to a bad experience and didn't raise it again. Not until a few months later, when I was in Ballarat in regional Victoria on the County Court circuit, working as one of the junior instructing solicitors. In the usual banter over dinner that night I started telling the QC on the same case the story about how Judge X had given me such a hard time that day in court. I'd barely started telling the story when he got that knowing smirk, almost identical to the partner's.

'I've heard this story ...' he said.

I thought one of his barrister friends must have been sniggering in court that day and that I was about to find out exactly how I'd screwed up.

'A group of us were at drinks in the bar and Judge X entertained us all with your story.'

'What?'

'Yeah. He said the highlight of his week was when a good-looking young brunette lawyer was before him on a simple adjournment matter. He asked her a string of questions he didn't need to ask – just so he could keep her on her feet and keep looking at her ...'

I'd been kicking myself for months over my apparent failure

to do the job, when it turned out my only mistake had been to be young and female.

*

'Dress for success' is a standard mantra for both men and women working in any profession. But when you look at the hundreds of articles with advice about what to wear to a job interview, or what to wear when doing a presentation to the board, they are mainly addressed to women.

For men, there's not much to say. The standard suit-and-tie uniform calls for little time. A wash-and-wear haircut, clean shirt, nice suit, polished shoes. Easy.

For women, it's complicated.

One day, after I had risen to senior ranks, I was in the room with other members of an executive team and board members from our parent company. A young woman was up against her peer male colleague, making a big presentation that meant one of them would be offered a position overseas. She was neck and neck with her male competitor in terms of presentation and delivery. Her content was far superior. But she didn't get the gig.

During the debrief, when she and her competitor left the room, the majority of those who sat around the table chose the guy, though none could really articulate why. Until one board member blurted out, 'Does she always look such a mess?' Embarrassed faces all started looking down at their papers. We quickly moved on.

He's right, I thought. *Though he could have been a tad more tactful.*

They had both worn jumpers, shirts and trousers. This was fine – it was a business casual everyday policy. But her jumper had highly visible food stains on it. Her pants hadn't seen an iron and her hair looked like it hadn't seen shampoo, let alone a hairbrush for a few days. Her shoes looked like her favourites – well-worn with scuffs. Her nails looked like she'd spent the weekend in the garden. She basically looked like she'd rolled out of bed and done that teenage thing of selecting clothes from the 'floordrobe'.

She was very despondent about the outcome, and she couldn't work out how she could have done better. After she'd asked her boss and others for feedback to no avail, she came to me. I gave her some constructive feedback, along the lines that you don't have to be a fashion plate, but you do have to be presentable … and not just for presentations. I told her about me turning up in my suit with Weet-Bix on the collar, courtesy of my toddler, and how I was genuinely grateful when a male colleague pointed it out to me before I entered a meeting. I advised her to always look like she made an effort, at least to be neat and tidy

She took my advice seriously. One year later a similar opportunity came up, and she got the gig.

Appearance matters, in all sectors, and it's worth paying attention to. Your appearance often has an effect on your sense of self, whether you're dressed in high fashion or simply dressed neatly. The feedback women receive about their appearance, though, is often anything but constructive – in fact, it is more often designed to be destructive. And almost always unsolicited.

In any role with a public profile, a woman's appearance takes on a gargantuan importance. And a disproportionate amount of time.

'Tell her white doesn't suit her, it makes her look even older than she is.'

'What's with her thick black hair?'

'She shouldn't wear so much make-up.'

'She needs more make-up.'

'She wore that same suit last week.'

'Why has she got so many different suits?'

These are just a small sample of the comments my staff would have to field about me during sitting weeks in parliament. I had a prominent position, seated directly behind then Prime Minister Malcolm Turnbull, and people from far and wide would take the time to pick up the phone, get through to my staff and complain. In real time.

My staff had to constantly field comments about the colour of my dark skin and hair – veiled reference to my Greek heritage. It happened so many times that my staffer grew tired of feigning the polite 'I'll pass your message on'. So once when a caller said, 'Tell your MP to stop using so much fake tan,' she calmly replied, 'I'll have you know that is my boss's natural skin colour, but thank you for your casual racism' before hanging up.

Once, a male MP got out of his seat during Question Time and walked down to where I was sitting (which meant we were both in full camera view) to show me a message he'd received along the lines of 'Tell that good looker to smile more.' My reaction was likely being watched by the person who'd sent the message in real time. The MP messenger looked up to the cameras, obviously wanting to indicate to his text messenger that he had taken the time to deliver this piece of worldly advice. I think at the time the foreign minister was at the despatch box talking about something very serious. I maintained my stoicism and listened intently – not for the cameras, but because I was doing my job.

Dressing for success can sometimes feel more like 'dressing for gendered abuse'. This is where sexism comes to the fore – sometimes subtly and sometimes in a brutally overt way. Sexism is used to diminish a woman or damage her reputation, whether she is in a position of power or seen to be challenging forces of power.

The greater the public profile of a successful woman, the deeper and more hostile the sexism can become. Particularly on social media – a forum which is not optional for these women but rather a professional imperative, be they a politician, journalist, sports star or celebrity. A study conducted by Gender Equity Victoria and the Media, Entertainment & Arts Alliance called *Don't Read the Comments,* about enhancing online safety for women working in the media, found that online abuse was often not only sexist but was also designed to silence women or do reputational harm.

The more my actions were seen to be challenging powerful forces and the more public my profile became, the more acute and brutal the gendered abuse became. Particularly from 'no caller ID' calls, on social media, and in coordinated letter-writing campaigns to my office and to the press. Most of it was so vile that my staff and I spent an inordinate amount of time filtering phone messages and deleting posts. When I became an independent, I received high level abuse and death threats classified as 'low level' by the police. On advice, we had to 'monitor' these messages, so the agonising process became a daily, if not hourly, ritual.

The expert advice that these comments were from my opponents and 'designed to mess with my head' was an understatement.

I noticed that two words kept popping up in the abusive comments: Shut. Up. They appeared in various forms. *Shut up Bitch. STFU, just shut up already. Shut up and go back to the kitchen. I'm sick of listening to you. Shut up & take your HRT.*

They were not all just unknown trolls and keyboard warriors. And believe it or not, many of them were happy to identify themselves. A quick internet search identified a number as party members and 'friends' of other party members. Their united aim was to silence me.

*

Just as I've always loved all things feminine since I was a little girl, I've also always been a feminist. Particularly given the 'you must get equal opportunities to your brother' insistence from my mother. I always simply thought that men and women should be equal, and I learnt early on that the only thing men might be better at, at least as far as I was concerned, was physical strength.

Before I entered the workplace I had been used to being judged purely on my achievements, not my looks. But from my first day on my very first job as a teenager selling Easter eggs in the shopping mall, the boss would tap me on my backside every time I walked past him after making a sale. Appearance and success are often toxically entwined for women.

Femininity and fashion are often called frivolous and they flag you as a 'girly girl' – the type of woman who can be dismissed with popular generalisations about women's weaknesses. Helen Lewis summarises the stereotypes well in her book, *Difficult Women*: 'Men are serious, women are silly. Men are rational, women are emotional. Men are strong, women are weak. Men are steadfast, women are fickle. Men are objective, women are subjective. Men are humanity, women are a subset of it. Men want sex, and women grant or withhold it. Women are looked at; men do the looking. When we're victims, it is hard to believe us.'

The same people who believe all this believe that women are not good leadership material. During another of my preselection interviews, one of the preselectors said, 'You seem too nice, too ladylike, not strong enough to be a good MP – so I can't vote for you.' He thought he was paying me a compliment.

There's no getting away from this, even if as a woman you eschew fashion and femininity – you're still likely to be called either too weak, or too strong. Or difficult. Any woman can run the risk of that accusation the moment she challenges or disagrees with something. Theresa May was famously described in an off-the-cuff remark by a former conservative chancellor as a 'bloody difficult woman'. In May's case, she managed to turn the slur around and wear it as a badge of honour: 'ready to do battle' in the context of the Brexit negotiations.

A difficult woman is almost always equated with a feminist woman. This might explain why many women, including those who are shining examples of women in leadership, are reluctant to say that they're a feminist, in case they might suddenly be seen as 'difficult'.

For a term about believing in equality, feminism is bizarrely divisive. I'm always stunned at the number of anti-feminists, men and women, who are still everywhere in workplace cultures, lurking about in the corridors of power. I wonder if that would change if more people understood the word, pure and simple, as a belief in equality of the sexes: socially, economically and politically.

The natural continuation of being anti-feminist is often the acceptance of sexism. But unlike feminism, sexism doesn't have a definition that could be confusing. It's clear. Sexism is sex-based prejudice, stereotyping or discrimination that underscores certain abuses of power. Sexism is the beast that lurks in the corner and rears its ugly head where power and women intersect.

When I made the decision in my early twenties to leave private legal practice and join the world of commerce as a corporate lawyer, I didn't leave because of the sexism. In fact, the corporate role was in the manufacturing sector, so some may assume it would have been like going from the frying pan into the fire. But what I experienced, even in the early years of my corporate career, further informed my belief that the corporate sector was ahead of the legal profession when it came to equality – largely because of the inbuilt structures of the different workplaces. Private legal practice is an entrenched, lineal hierarchy, where mainly men sit in the partner ranks and in the judiciary.

I remember once attending a boardroom lunch that was evenly split between corporate general counsels (a mix of men and women) and senior partners of law firms (all men). During the lunch, most of the senior partners of the law firms repeatedly expressed astonishingly outdated and blinkered views in relation to workplace equality. Afterwards, my corporate colleagues and I had to go out for a drink just to decompress.

The image problem of feminism is particularly acute in politics – a world where, in fact, it should be a core item for discussion. On more than one occasion I was called a 'leftie feminist'– as if being a feminist necessarily means you have leftist political views. Male leaders are rarely asked whether they're a feminist or not – and I suspect if they were asked, a lot of them would be stumped for an answer. No doubt many think 'it's a women's thing'.

At the end of the day, though, as Emma Watson summed it up: 'If you stand for equality, then you're a feminist – I'm sorry to tell you.'

*

On a journey to run for one of the most powerful positions in the world, as the president of the United States, Hillary Clinton encountered extraordinary sexism, including from Donald Trump himself. In her book *What Happened?* Clinton discusses the balancing act required for women in politics, which I believe can apply across the board, in all sectors. 'If we're too tough, we're unlikeable. If we're too soft, we're not cut out for the big leagues. If we work too hard, we're neglecting our families. If we put our families first, we're not serious about work. If we have a career but no children, there's something wrong with us and vice versa.'

When it comes to women and leadership, likeability is a term that comes up far too often.

I've sat through many board-level performance reviews of high achievers. On one particular occasion we were having a discussion around the table about a woman who ticked all the boxes to be a high-calibre emerging leader. Someone said he'd heard she'd once 'lost it' with a fellow employee who took her car parking spot, which had made her late for a meeting. A whole five minutes was devoted to a circuitous discussion about how she could have 'handled the car park situation differently'; words such as 'overemotional' and 'aggressive' were starting to be used. Group think was taking over.

But then a male colleague spoke: 'Are we seriously considering tanking this woman's entire career because she told off that idiot for taking her parking spot? He's a serial offender – does it to everyone across the company. At least she gave him "in the moment" clear feedback and explained the impact of his actions meaning she would miss an important meeting.'

As this point I chimed in: 'Yeah, like imagine if her name was Joe with an "e".'

As in the case of that famous 2003 Columbia Business School 'Heidi vs Howard' study, if all the key achievements of Jo were outlined in the performance review document, but we put Joe's name on it for the year, I suspected the 'car park issue' wouldn't have seen the light of day.

A slightly stunned, humble-pie eating silence blanketed the room.

Jo got a gold star performance review.

These biases are deeply entrenched, which means we can all

slip into them without meaning to from time to time. If both men and women work to remain aware of them and call them out when we see them, it will help in big ways and small. The male colleague at that meeting put Jo's career on the track it deserved to be on.

The boardrooms, the meeting room tables, and our parliamentary chambers need men and women to be active feminists and to manage sexist behaviour where they see it. Everyone needs to do everything they can to balance the success and likeability correlation.

It is key that leaders embrace and appreciate the differences in masculinity and femininity, rather than denigrating them. It's important that you make your appearance and presentability work for you in whatever way enables you to be yourself and makes you feel more powerful.

For me, it's always been important to take care of my appearance. Not just for the aesthetics. But because it was a form of armour that made me feel stronger on the inside.

For my preselection, which is invariably a bruising or at least intense experience, no matter your political allegiance, I bought myself a new suit. It was a strong, deep-blue colour with nice simple lines and a zipper up the front. I wore it with a pair of earrings that my son had given me the previous Mother's Day (they had been on the wish list). I won my preselection. And so, it was an easy decision to wear the suit and earrings on the night of the election win, and again on my first speech to the parliament. I dubbed them my lucky suit and earrings.

Throughout my time in politics, I would put lipstick on before a radio interview. Even when I did the interviews on the phone in the privacy of my office, I knew I was wearing it, and it gave me an extra bit of courage.

In the lead-up to making what became known as my resignation speech in the federal parliament, I'd gone through a roller-coaster of emotions, including feeling under siege, mentally exhausted and like I just wanted to close the door and hide away for a few months.

But I knew I had to do everything I could to muster my courage. This was going to be a battle. A battle I picked. A battle I saw as part of my contribution to my continuing advocacy for gender equality. A battle which would challenge the most powerful forces in the country. This was another one of those intense moments and I needed my armour. I wore my lucky suit and earrings.

I was wearing them when I rose in the chamber and waited for the call from the Speaker to make my 'personal statement on indulgence'. With resolute focus, I said to myself, *I've got this.*

Chapter 3

Never too young

'Welcome home' said the CEO, as he was walking past my office.

I barely got to say 'thank you' before he'd gone. But I was quietly glad our eye contact lasted only a few seconds. Any longer, and he would have seen me tear up in response to his two-word greeting. I looked blindly down at the papers on my desk to conceal my face and my tears, which would have been readily seen by anyone passing by my glass-walled office.

Those two words evoked a totally unexpected surge of emotion in me, as I had only been just over a couple of months into this new job when I unexpectedly had to take an extended period of sick leave. Those two words made me feel a warm sense of belonging and emotional support, even though I barely knew the CEO at that point. The longest conversation I'd had with him was during the job interview.

I was the new kid on the block. 'Kid' being the operative word – I'd even heard it used in legal circles upon the announcement of my appointment to this new role: a big general counsel and company secretary role for a blue-chip company.

It had been widely known in Melbourne's legal fraternity that this job was up for grabs. Prestigious and challenging, it was the kind of job that was rare as hen's teeth back then. There was little movement in general counsel jobs, and when they did become available, lawyers with years of experience or established senior associates and junior partners would go for them. The interview process was intense, comprehensive and fiercely competitive. After eleven interviews – all after-hours – and a slew of referee checks, I got the gig.

Only a year earlier, my then boss had persuaded me that it was a good opportunity to nominate for the voluntary role of committee secretary of the Victorian Corporate Lawyers Association. Aside from being only one of two women in this voluntary association, I was the youngest of everyone. In my twenties, albeit my late twenties, just looking at the others around the table at meetings made me feel too young for the role. Nonetheless it was a great learning experience.

After one of those committee meetings, and just after it became public that I'd secured this new job, we all went on to an event that the committee had organised. It was there that I overheard two middle-aged male lawyers talking to each other, clearly oblivious that I was within earshot.

'I mean, she's just a kid.'

'Yeah, and why on earth the recruiters would put her forward in the first place I have no idea. Though she is a woman,' he added with a familiar sarcastic tone.

I found out subsequently that one of the two men engrossed in this analysis of the recruitment process had applied for the role as well. Apparently he hadn't even made the shortlist.

Around the same time, I was at a corporate lawyers' post-conference drinks event when the archetypal cliché of the older male lawyer (the type who fancies himself as the arrogant, handsome maverick Harvey Specter from *Suits*) sidled up to me. Hugging his beer and ogling me at the same time, he was physically unable to hide his arrogance as he said 'Congratulations.' He added, in a part-condescending and part-sleazy tone, 'You're so young.'

Despite the rigorous recruitment process, despite all the encouraging feedback, a stream of similar events fed the nagging voice of self-doubt that became increasingly loud in my head.

In the early days of settling into the new job, during my first executive team meeting, I looked around the boardroom table and realised all of the others on the CEO leadership team were in their forties and fifties. I've no doubt my reluctance to speak up at these meetings wasn't just a case of my being new, but also because of the casual ageist comments that enhanced my self-consciousness about my relative youth, compared to their age and experience.

I began to think that maybe I'd oversold myself by putting myself forward for the job in the first place.

It's often cited as an absolute truth that women, unlike men, are concerned that they need to have all the requirements for a job before they even apply for it. In the media, in the workplace and in social settings, people will bring it up as if it's based on a study or empirical evidence. That evidence doesn't in fact exist. The truth is more likely that some people, both men *and* women, are more inclined to talk up their credentials more than others. But this urban myth does tie in nicely with how we think women should behave.

Nonetheless, in the early days of that job, I heard my inner critic, loud and clear. I tried to counter this and lift my confidence with traditional self-affirmations. *You were the best person for the job*, *Be more confident and assertive* and *Speak up in meetings*. You name the advice, I'd heard it or read it somewhere.

Although I diligently learned the ropes of my new job, my imposter syndrome grew stronger and the same words kept popping back into my head.

I'm too young. Too inexperienced. I'm going to get found out.

*

Despite all this, the timing of my getting the job coincided with my starting to really feel like I was living the dream. I had a new partner (who is now my husband), after having left a marriage that I dubbed the mistake of my youth. I was travelling to places I'd dreamed about. Enjoying holidays and good food. Enjoying life.

When I got this great job, I threw everything into it, and tried to balance my life with the new stress that comes with a new job. One of those stress relievers for me has always been exercise. One day, my partner and I were jogging together on the track around Melbourne's Botanical Gardens, known by locals as 'the Tan', when he noticed a small lump in my neck, which I'd already known was there. I'd had it checked out a year earlier, and the specialist had said it was nothing to worry about – 'just a cyst'. But at my partner's request, and because I still felt uneasy about its presence, I made an appointment with the same specialist to get it looked at again.

'I've told you. It's just a cyst.' I was relieved, he didn't say he suspected the other C-word. 'If I were you, I'd just get it drained every so often,' he said as he did just that – syringing out the fluid.

I saw him standing at the sink, ready to dispose of the minuscule amount of fluid housed in the syringe, and I suddenly blurted out, 'Yeah, but can you please just send it to pathology this time?'

He looked at me quizzically. I felt young and stupid. Who was

I to challenge a specialist in a white coat? I felt the need to apologise for being so paranoid. But I was trusting my gut. My instinct told me something was wrong.

He rolled his eyes, smiling at my over-the-top request, but agreed. The fluid he'd syringed out was put in a bottle and sent to pathology. It was saved from going down the sink.

And that saved my life.

Within two days, I found myself sitting in front of another doctor who said, 'You've got thyroid cancer. We don't know if it's Cancer A or Cancer B. If it's Cancer A … you won't be here by Christmas.' I pretty much stopped hearing him at that point, but he went on. 'If it's Cancer B, it's totally curable. We won't know which it is for ten days. We have to open you up to find out, but it will have to be after the Easter break because I'm going away.'

With the efficiency of someone in a hurry, he put his pen down and closed his notebook. I felt like he was just short of calling out 'Next', as they do at the supermarket deli.

As I looked back at him from the door, I remember mumbling, 'Well, let's hope for Cancer B then.'

Thoughts started racing through my mind as I exited the doctor's office. My legs felt like they were borne down by weights and barely took me to where my car was parked. The drive home from the clinic was more dangerous than the diagnosis. The view of the road was clouded by my tears. Thoughts and questions occasionally pierced the fog in my mind. *How do I tell my loved ones? My partner? My boss!*

I started stressing about my job. *I've only been in this new job for a few months. Do I give it up? I'll have to take time off. They'll probably sack me. I should just quit anyway, I might be dead in a few months.* And even, albeit fleetingly, *Maybe I should just take my own life …*

Then the myriad of thoughts distilled down to one thought: *I may not have time. Time to live my life.*

And then, *I'm too young.*

During that predominantly dark period, my feeling that everything was out of control was immense. One of the things I *could* control was who I told about my diagnosis. I didn't want to share my story broadly, and I rarely shared it for many years after. I feared that I wouldn't be able to bear the burden and pain of people's responses to the word 'cancer'.

Back then, social media didn't represent your circle of influence as it does now, but I can tell you that if it had happened today, I wouldn't have shared the news there. I still feel uneasy for any people, particularly young people, who 'overshare' personal matters on social media as if meeting the expectations of others. Always in a crisis (whether personal or otherwise), it's important to focus on what you can control, rather than what you can't – and that includes communications. Announcing personal news to a forum of strangers can introduce an additional layer of chaos and unpredictable outcomes to an already difficult situation.

I limited my news to my loved ones, my closest inner circle of friends and a few selected work colleagues – including the CEO. It was that concentrated support that helped me hold it together.

My partner, the great love of my life, was there by my side every minute. Only two weeks after I had first been to see the specialist – but two weeks that felt like a lifetime in terms of the emotions I had been through and the conversations I'd had – they put me under general anaesthetic and cut out the lump on my neck.

When I came to and opened my eyes a few hours later apparently my first question was whether I was going to grow old with my partner.

'Yes', said the specialist. And without another word I fell back into my deep post-general-anaesthetic-induced slumber.

*

About a year later, under another highly selective process, I had the opportunity to attend a prestigious executive leadership development program. One of the exercises required all the attendees to fill out a confidential survey, placing a tick in the box to identify how many 'stress events' we'd had in the immediately preceding two years.

Break-up of a long-term relationship ending in divorce – tick. Moving to a new house (three times) – tick, tick, tick. Death of a loved one (my only living grandparent) – tick. Serious illness – tick. Marriage – tick. New job – tick.

A score of over two ticks 'needed attention', said the facilitator. My score was embarrassingly off the charts.

One of my fellow attendees twenty years my senior, who was self-conscious about his score as he'd 'had a bit going on' in his life, nosily took a peek at my score – which was of course meant to be confidential. With genuine concern, he whispered 'Holy shit … what happened to you? You're too bloody young.'

Often when people have gone through a near-death event, they will get a different life perspective. They will say that they now value every day, or they're thankful for every moment. It often takes a crisis or something like it to realise that your life counts. That you are enough. That you are not just defined by your job and your achievements, but also by your ability to empathise and connect with others. People write books and make inspirational speeches about this, which isn't surprising. After all, how many times do we all say, 'Life's too short'?

What I learnt after my cancer scare was that I was not too

young for the big things in life, whether good or bad. The most important lesson I learnt was that you cannot build a life, a career or a reputation based on what you *will* do – it has to be based on what you *are* doing.

From that moment in the doctor's clinic, I learnt to believe in myself and the decisions I made, and to rely on my instincts. Throughout my life since then, my instincts have rarely let me down. If I'm ever ambivalent about something, even having done a complex pros-cons analysis, the old 'go with your gut' approach always takes me down the right path.

I also learnt to appreciate the gift of time, to make career changes, and to not always take the safe path. I made sure my job title didn't define or pigeonhole what I could do, but instead pushed myself to think outside the box. I learnt to ask myself questions like *What have you got to lose? What's the worst thing that can happen?* And, the most important question of all: *Even though I might not have positional power yet, can I use my personal power to make a difference?*

I became less afraid to speak out on matters that I had previously considered outside my remit. I led diversity councils and committees working on workplace cultural issues – such as gender and cultural equality. I led different change and transformation projects, and I executed new ideas. I was always lucky to work in organisations that valued teamwork and leadership accountability.

Dacher Keltner, professor of psychology at the University of California Berkeley and author of *The Power Paradox*, argues that power is given to leaders by those in the team. He describes how power is given to leaders who are sharing, who pass on their wisdom, demonstrate empathy and who are willing to brainstorm and embrace a shared goal, both within their workplaces and the greater community.

One of those new ideas that I pursued was an overhaul of my corporate employer's philanthropic program. My initial job description in this role meant that my oversight was strictly confined to the administrative governance side of the company's philanthropy program, but I couldn't help observing that this program had evolved into little more than a routine annual administrative process. The same budget was distributed to the same places (usually 'favourite charities' of former managers) in a fragmented, ad hoc manner each year, without any active consideration or involvement on the part of staff. Although outside my remit, I had an idea to overhaul the program, make it more focussed and meaningful, and align it with our business' values. I wanted to bring new energy and life into it by identifying key charities and causes to channel our budget into, which would be reassessed regularly, while encouraging employee involvement through volunteerism, with the company's support.

The traditional pushback came from the older, long-serving employees along the lines that they'd always done it that way. 'If it ain't broke, don't fix it,' one literally said. The resistance was so strong that I started thinking I should drop it. But the ultimate call was that of the same CEO who had given me his two-word welcome home message some years earlier. I knew from the time of my interviews for the job and that early gesture of compassion that he was very much an empathetic leader.

I knew he might still agree with his other direct reports that I should drop it – after all, I was going out on a limb with this new-fangled idea. But he loved it. 'We need new fresh ideas from our younger staff. Keep going until someone tells you to stop. If anyone tells you to stop, come and see me, and I'll make sure you can keep going,' he said.

And so I led a small team who were as passionate as I was about creating a more meaningful program. One of our first events was as a corporate participant in a huge charitable Christmas party being held for 5000 child attendees who were socially or intellectually disadvantaged in some way. Because we worked in a food business, we'd set up a kitchen where the children could decorate a gingerbread biscuit, under the supervision of one of our team members.

I was there the whole day leading the proceedings, and at one point I looked over and noticed the mum of one of the children crying while watching her son doing the activity. Some of my team members were high-fiving him and supporting him. 'Is everything okay?' I asked, putting my hand on the mother's shoulder.

Her son was a perfectly healthy young boy. But you're never too young for something terrible to happen. Only months earlier, he had been climbing a tree when he had fallen from a significant height, causing residual brain damage. The doctors had said he would improve by doing as many cognitive activities as possible. He'd resisted doing them, as he was embarrassed by his disability, and had then become despondent that he'd never improve. His emotional and tearful mum explained to me, while simultaneously apologising for her tears, that this was the first time she'd seen him smile and actively do something and that it had given her hope that he would get better. We waived the one-gingerbread biscuit limit for this boy. He did six.

The program transformation was regarded as so successful that it was rolled out internationally, and my fellow team members and I were rewarded and recognised on a global corporate level. But the real power behind its success was the buy-in we'd fostered from the wider employee group, from having a company-wide vote to determine which charities we would focus on, to creating flexible work conditions that allowed them to help out with the charities both on company and personal time. And certainly my feeling of achievement was strongest on that day when we watched the young boy decorating six biscuits under the proud gaze of his mum.

My encounter with cancer in my late twenties had forced me to value the gift of time in my life. In my work, I began to build a career that reflected my own values. What was more, by trusting myself and doing things the way I thought they should be done, I was able to prove how capable I was in my role and as a leader, even though I may have been thought of by some as just 'a kid'.

*

Every decade we age tends to be automatically marked as an important milestone. Age discrimination isn't reserved for those of an older or 'certain' age. It also isn't just restricted to what other people think of you – it can come from within and cloud what you think of yourself. But neither of these discriminations, from others or self-inflicted, are helped by a workplace culture that feeds into this entrenched ageism.

When I was a bit older, in my thirties and forties, it seemed to me that the human resources industry would never have survived if it weren't for the supposed puzzle of young people. Conferences and workshops popped up everywhere guiding the more senior manager on how to manage these people born after 1980: those pesky Gen Ys and Gen Z'ers. In conference after conference, they were labelled everything from entitled to narcissistic.

I recall feeling really annoyed at one conference session I had to attend when the speaker, a much older male who was not far from retirement, was lumping this age group together in one kind of 'tech savvy but lazy' stereotype. I sat there thinking of the brilliant young people who reported to me, who were undoubtedly tech savvy but anything but lazy.

The long span of our lifetimes is likely going to mean that people live and work differently than their forebears, as the world, our technology and our cultures change, especially in the wake of the pandemic – but generational warfare is clearly not the answer. The 'OK boomer' catchphrase used by teenagers and young adults to dismiss or mock attitudes of those older than them is probably born of a frustration that their young voices aren't being heard or represented.

Regardless of the stereotypes that develop about each new generation, the 'I'm too young' thought process is still alive and well. A recent article about generational differences in the workplace for the *Harvard Business Review* referenced research that showed that 'Younger workers believed that others would see them in a more negative manner than they actually did ("unmotivated" and "irresponsible")'. The research also found that, when it came to people's prejudices regarding age, these judgements were not based on any proven biological or behavioural differences between age groups, but rather people's *beliefs* that those differences existed. What people saw as proof of age-related competence or incompetence was all in their heads.

A strategy that has proven to be effective in countering this ageism is engaging colleagues in collaborative tasks that involve people of all ages working towards a shared goal.

The biggest shared goal of our time remains the battle to save our planet. Alarmingly, the pandemic's grip has delayed sensible policy discussion about this enormous pending crisis. The science shows that the black summer bushfires are a taste of what the future looks like if those in power don't stop playing political football with climate change and start taking meaningful climate action now. Being an eyewitness to the ways energy policy was used as a tool in the power plays of MPs and leaders, and how that led to the destruction of good government rather than the implementation of meaningful climate change action, was nothing short of disturbing.

It's not alarmist to call this a climate emergency. When you're short of time, when you have to act quickly, that's called an emergency. We are squandering the gift of time. As Michael Mann, professor of atmospheric science said, we must 'take the earliest exit possible off the fossil fuel highway'.

The School Strike 4 Climate was an incredible display of the power of young people – no doubt many of whom were inspired by Swedish teenage environmental activist Greta Thunberg. The strike coincided with the beginnings of the election campaign in 2019. This was a politically inconvenient time for both the major parties, who each issued the same negative political message for different political ideological reasons: the students should strike on the weekend, not on a school day. Both of them missed the point of the core tactic to get global attention. The genius of it was that it was a *school* strike.

'They should be in school.' 'They should be learning history.' The message points from parliament came thick and fast.

But these children were making history.

In a review of the documentary *I Am Greta*, Kate Douglas poignantly reminds us that 'children are not just adults-in-waiting: their experiences and voices are significant in themselves and worthy of our attention … Reading young people's stories recognises their citizenship and the vital role children play in the political world.'

The strike was attended by millions of people across Australia. Never before have I seen firsthand the energy, passion and commitment of so many young people join so exuberantly together with people of all ages, from all generations, united by a shared goal.

I met so many of those people during my independent campaign that year, from teachers to grandparents. I met students from as young as ten through to those in Year 12, all of whom articulated clearly and passionately that they wanted a safer future.

One of the students who I met was an eleven-year-old girl heading into the climate strike in the city, accompanied by her grandmother, because her parents were working. I asked her why she was going to the strike. 'I have to go with Nana because Mum says I'm not allowed to go into the city by myself. But if we don't save our planet from getting too hot, we won't have beautiful countryside, and it's bad for all the animals. We won't have anything.'

I replied, 'Your mum's right that you're too young to go on the train into the city by yourself, but how lovely is it that your nan is taking you – because you're never too young to stand for what's important.'

'Or too old,' quipped the girl's grandmother.

'Of course, or too old,' I repeated, and we exchanged looks that expressed multi-generational solidarity.

It was incredible to witness the way young voices were made that much stronger and more potent when listened to and supported by those older: multiple generations, working together, to support future ones. That collective unit is the most powerful voice there is.

In the beginning of her campaign, passers-by barely acknowledged the young Greta Thunberg; now she's heard around the globe. Not everyone needs to aspire to leading a global climate change action, but all young people can ensure they are listened to based on what they are doing right now, not just what they will do 'when they grow up'!

*

Australia needs young women to aspire to positions of power, and that won't happen if young voices aren't heard.

There's a prevailing belief that someone is 'too inexperienced' if they're in their early-to-mid-twenties. But by their twenties, people have twenty-plus years of life experience – both the experience of life itself and what they've learnt in study and work so far. In fact, a lot of people have started accumulating valuable skills in their casual work, be it waiting tables or working on the checkout. Communication skills, decision-making, planning, having empathy, getting the job done, coming up with new ideas – all are things that can happen in casual jobs.

People are never too young to challenge what people say – so challenging the 'no experience' dismissal is always a good one. Prospective employers, recruiters or other equivalents should ask the question, 'What about your life experience in the last five years ... can you tell me about that?'

I met a young woman recently for a coffee as she was wanting to pick my brain about what she should do next. A new and very different job opportunity had come her way, but she felt torn between what she thought she should do, what she wanted to do, and what she was doing. She described her dilemma as if she were an adult-in-waiting. She thought she was too young to take any risk and that she should follow the path and plan she'd outlined in her mind when she was studying at university.

I said to her, 'If you can't try new things when you're young, then when do you think you can?'

I recalled a rare reflective moment back when I was working at the private law firm, when I'd started suspecting that perhaps it wasn't right for me. After all my work, all my perfectionism and precision planning, all my striving to get the job and continue on the career pathway I'd envisaged, I was quietly devastated to feel this doubt. I tried to block the thoughts out of my head, but they wouldn't leave. As I looked ahead on that pathway, I found I wasn't looking forward to what I could see. Sometimes I saw people a few years older than me getting excited about being promoted to senior associate, striving to make senior partner and get a corner office, but I couldn't share their excitement. I thought I'd made a fundamental mistake with my plan. But making a sideways change to corporate law ended up opening so many doors to me.

I explained to her my firm belief that there's never a 'right' age to try new things, change your mind, accept new challenges. That although she'd planned and studied and internalised a set career path, she shouldn't feel guilty about going through a different door. Doors will be opened and closed throughout your career and working life. Sometimes, sliding door moments can make it even more complicated, and opportunity comes at an inconvenient time. And sometimes you might just want to take a peek inside a door and then it leads you somewhere else completely.

In the words of model/newsreader/organic farmer/climate warrior Patrice Newell, someone I've long admired, 'Life should be *full* of career changes. Forever and ever. I feel for young people today saying I don't know what I really want to do … you don't have to, life's a *surprise*, go with the flow and the feelings of the day.'

I once offered one of my direct reports a promotion. It meant a slight salary increase and a massive status increase. She said no. She was not ready for it: 'too young', 'too inexperienced'. She said she'd 'never done that sort of work before'. She was in fact young and inexperienced, but I wouldn't have offered her the job if I didn't think she could do it. She's a highly intelligent fast learner. The conversation went for about a half hour in which I challenged her decline. But she seemed adamant, and at the same time confused in the confidence I had in her.

I remembered I'd been sitting exactly where she was some ten years earlier, and I shared with her that I had been petrified that I wouldn't know what I was doing – the person who offered me the opportunity had had absolute confidence that I could do it, and sometimes you've got to let an outside person quiet that critic on your inside. I accepted her decline, but prompted her to ask herself two questions after she left the meeting: 'What have I got to lose?' and 'Why not?'

Within fifteen minutes, she was back in my office. 'Can we just replay that conversation?'

I was surprised and delighted by her fast self-reflection. I could sense in her tone alone that she'd had a change of mind.

To feel you're not too young for a role, particularly a leadership role, means having a healthy regard for the gift of time and trusting your instinct and self-belief. It doesn't mean having an overinflated view of your abilities and faking your experience. And it absolutely does mean that you should never underestimate the value of executive or management experience. That is something you absolutely cannot fake.

One friend said she took the opportunity of board appointments too young, in her thirties, and should have got more executive experience up her sleeve first. It's better to consider this as a kind of chicken-and-egg scenario, rather than a sequence issue. There's no fixed template, and it's far better to relax and accept that everyone has to start somewhere. No matter the number of courses, training or mentorships that you do, nothing beats just diving in.

This also means tapping into your reserves of courage from time to time. It's not unusual for younger people coming up through the ranks to be self-conscious about contributing and feel intimidated by older people in the room. But you just have to push through that discomfort, with courage.

One other thing you can never do enough of, no matter your age, is ask questions. Most young adults haven't had direct experience of a toddler going through the 'why' stage. This is probably a good thing – I still remember how exhausting it could become. But asking questions is a natural part of the growing, learning and developing phases in life, at any age. Asking what, why and how is a fundamental base for trying new things and experiencing new challenges. Without asking questions, we don't give ourselves the best chance of reaching our full potential as workers and leaders – or as people.

I once received a piece of not-so-worldly advice from a CEO who honestly believed the 'unwritten rule' of the corporate world that after six months in a new job, you have to stop asking questions like a new person – his view being that 'You should know it all after that time.'

Perhaps because my legal training involved always asking questions, I took that piece of advice with a grain of salt. But particularly when I was younger, I'd still find myself holding back and not asking the questions that were bothering me. Then I began to notice that, on the occasions when someone else in the meeting did ask the question I'd been thinking, I could tell I wasn't the only person who pricked up their ears thinking, *Mmm, I was wondering about that.*

I've worked with or alongside countless leaders in my corporate career, on a massive variety of different issues and topics. By far and away, the best leaders are the ones that ask the questions – particularly when there's a crisis. Good managers will reassure that 'there's no such thing as a dumb question', but great leaders really mean it and will take the time to explain or talk through something with their colleagues.

In every workplace, in every discipline, in every situation, young voices can make a huge difference. I find it so disheartening when I hear people, especially those with a public profile, say, simply because of their negative experiences, that they wouldn't recommend that young women aspire to leadership positions in certain sectors. It's a way of saying, 'Look what happened to me when I tried to play that power game – it would have been better to stay silent.' But it's always important to remember that your own perspectives, abilities and lived experiences will add value, in small ways and large, not only to your own life but to the lives of others.

In Australia we have recently seen an emerging power like no other. Young women, who historically would have fitted strongly into the category of the powerless with respect to gendered violence, sexism and misogyny, are speaking out for the generations after them. The generations *before* them have privately and silently experienced their hurt and anxiety – not because they were any less brave, but because of feelings of guilt, shame and fear imposed on them by the powerful. Still, the government is trying to manage this as a political issue, not an issue of humanity, in a way that seems very old-fashioned – like grandparents in their eighties and nineties refusing to use mobile phones and new technology. It's not working. They have to address this with real solutions. And the best way to start is to listen and act on the proposals of young people.

One leader I worked with used to have a little framed question on his desk facing anyone who would come in his office: 'Are you part of the problem or part of the solution?' You're never too young to be asked that question. Or to ask it of yourself.

Chapter 4

Power and prejudice

It was 26 January 2017. I was on the stage at a citizenship ceremony. These are conducted by local governments, but involve all tiers of government – including MPs, who, as part of the official proceedings, give the certificates and congratulatory wishes to the new Australian citizens. I was the federal MP for one of the most multicultural electorates in the country (where over a hundred languages other than English are spoken every day). At one moment, while looking out to the audience, I felt I could almost visibly see the raft of emotions on the faces before me. Excitement, gratitude, pride and happiness all shone back at me.

A Welcome to Country was conducted by an Aboriginal Elder, after which several speeches were made, including my own, which acknowledged the importance and honour of citizenship. The last speaker, also an MP, began her speech by saying that this day, Australia Day, should be known as Invasion Day. Her direct acknowledgement of ongoing injustice created a palpable change of atmosphere in the room. It was a reminder of the constant, deep and visceral tension in our country characterised by racism and prejudice.

Australia is unique – a multicultural nation, an immigrant nation and one with 60,000 years of history through its First Nations people. It is not defined by race, religion or cultural tradition. But although often hailed as one of the most successful multicultural nations in the world, racism and prejudice overlays Australian history, starting with the British colonisation of Indigenous Australia and continuing with waves of immigration, multiculturalism and the tensions of modern-day Australia. The aspiration towards a deep collective identity has always been a complex and vexed issue in our country. If mutual respect is absent, discrimination floods in, resulting in division rather than the unity we strive for.

As a politician, I always loved attending school assemblies on Harmony Day – a day which celebrates our multiculturalism. But many Australians who, like me, have non-Anglo migrant heritage, have found that harmony is sometimes only a thin veneer.

It doesn't help when we have high-profile national leaders and commentators who forget their higher duty of care as public figures, and instead spout completely vile commentary under the false premise that we have unfettered free speech in this country, or that 'it's just a joke', or that 'if' they caused offence, they 'didn't mean to'.

The flagship Greek–Australian newspaper, the *Neos Kosmos*, reported on my maiden speech as 'a heartfelt plea, asking the Australian parliament, and Australia itself, to reaffirm its commitment to overcome bigotry and prejudice in all their guises.' The night before my speech, Pauline Hanson said in her speech when she was re-elected in the Senate, 'In my first speech ... I said we were in danger of being "swamped by Asians" ... now we are in danger of being "swamped by Muslims".'

But racism and prejudice are not confined to media and public figures – they are present in our schools, our communities and our workplaces every day.

Sadly, these experiences usually start in childhood. Indigenous ABC journalist Miriam Corowa talks about a 'hardwired insecurity … an ingrained sensibility acquired during a childhood in which my brown skin often marked me out as different and inferior.'

My own childhood experiences of prejudice had the power to stymie my confidence in just being myself. I was born in Australia and so was my mother. Although both my parents were of Greek heritage, we had the life of a pretty typical Aussie suburban family. We always spoke English at home (though I did go to Greek school, which means I can read, write and speak Greek, albeit not very well). While we occasionally enjoyed the delights of Greek food and functions, we did all the things Aussie kids did: play cricket on the street, bus to the local beach on summer days, and eat fish and chips as a Friday night treat. There were only two overt things that gave away my Greek heritage, both inherited from my father: my dark looks and my family name (which we often anglicised, as Mum would say it was 'just easier'). These were enough to make my 'identity' conspicuous.

I remember when a boy in primary school randomly turned around during a sports game and spat the words at me, 'Wog, go back to your home country.'

I didn't know the meaning of the word 'wog', so the first thing I did when I got home from school that day was go into my brother's room and take the dictionary down off the bookshelf. There it was. Incredulously, I read the definition over and over. 'Someone of dark skin who is foreign to the land on which he lives.'

I had been hurt by the boy's aggressive, nasty tone – like I'd done something wrong. But when I found out the meaning of the word, I really felt singled out, ugly, scared and very alone. I felt conspicuous, in a negative way. I also didn't know what he meant by 'home country'. I didn't know any country in the world other than Australia as my home.

Many years later, in the early stage of my career, I was in the CBD office of one of Australia's biggest recruiting firms, nervously sitting opposite the recruiter as he was flicking through job opportunities. I'd responded to an ad where they'd specifically stated that they had opportunities for lawyers who had '1st or 2nd Year PQE' (post-qualification experience).

'Oh, here's one that could be an opportunity.' He started to read the brief more closely and then stopped midway and spoke. 'Look, actually, that won't work – I know they want a *young man.* Not a *Greek girl.*'

And there it was right there. The intersection. Sexism and racial prejudice combined and summed up in a few words: man vs girl, Australian vs Greek. It was the first moment where I realised that both my gender *and* my ethnicity were potential blocks to my career trajectory – and they were things over which I had no control.

Around the same time, I was talking to a director who had adult children my age. When I told him my brother is a doctor, he said, 'Wow. A doctor and a lawyer. You see, there it is, you kids from a migrant background – you're thankful and you appreciate your opportunities because you have that migrant work ethic. You work hard and you're successful. My kids are useless. They've had everything ...' and he went on, detailing his personal wealth while rationalising about why he thought his children were duds.

I'm sure that, in a perverse way, he thought he was paying me a compliment – that I was to be admired for having mythically emerged from the depths of a working-class migrant background to become 'something more' – and didn't stop to consider the prejudice he was displaying by suggesting I was the way I was simply because I had Greek heritage, and implying that I was not really Australian. I just let it pass – including when he mentioned that he and his wife had migrated from the UK, which meant his kids had more 'migrant heritage' than me, even if not in his Anglo-Saxon mind.

Ming Long, the chair of AMP Capital Funds Management, has described her encounter with the 'bamboo ceiling', and how, in order to get to her position, she's had to overcome the deep biases with which people in business meet an Asian-Australian woman. 'If you walk into a room with investors or bankers or whatever, you're walking in as an Asian woman, and you have opinions and you're loud and you have a voice in that meeting – that's not necessarily the stereotype they have in their mind. I'm not going into a meeting to take notes … I'm going to express my opinion, share and argue points. Some people are not used to seeing women do that, especially Asian women doing that.' Long says that she had to become more extroverted and that her Australian accent 'makes Aussies feel more comfortable' – even though, as she says, 'The whole point about diversity is the value of the difference you bring.'

During my time in the corporate world, a work colleague of mine who is third generation Chinese-Australian was once asked by the senior manager in one of those excruciating 'getting to know each other' round tables, 'Where are you from?'

She replied deadpan, 'Melbourne.'

I laughed out loud. The manager went bright red.

I heard a story of a young doctor, Australian-born with migrant heritage, who was taking the blood pressure of a patient in hospital. The patient looked at her name badge suspiciously and asked, 'Where are you from, Dr ... I can't pronounce your name?' Australia. 'Where are your parents from?' Australia. 'Where are your grandparents from?' Australia. The patient became visibly irritated. 'Don't be rude – you're different, you know what I mean!'

Overt signs that make you ostensibly different can be as simple as an accent or a name. One CEO I worked for would always take the time to check the pronunciation of the surname of individuals before giving out awards or prizes to them; it showed his inherent respect.

When taking my husband's surname, one thing I hadn't anticipated was how much easier life would become with a one-syllable Anglo surname. Gone were the days of correcting people's pronunciation, and even more significantly, I found I encountered less prejudice generally. But I couldn't escape it entirely. Once, newly married, I introduced myself to an American expat at a function. She slowly repeated 'Banks', and then said 'But you look *different.* Where are you from?'

Channelling my Chinese-Australian work colleague's sense of humour, I said 'Melbourne.' And then added, pointing to my British expat husband, 'He's the dual citizen.'

*

My happy place has long been at our home on the Mornington Peninsula – especially when extended family and friends visit. But on this day, despite being surrounded by the warmth of family, love and an open fire, and the squeals of my young children playing with their cousins in another room, the dark clouds and bleakness of the weather also defined the mood inside our home.

My father was dying of terminal cancer. He didn't have long – maybe a couple of months. He, my brother and I sat around the fire, generally chitchatting, studiously avoiding talking about Dad's illness, but the atmosphere brought on by the quiet stoicism and sadness of two adult children about to lose their father was palpable.

My older brother, like me, is hugely proud of being an Australian with Greek heritage. For forty-plus years he has cared for the patients of all backgrounds in his GP practice. He was describing to Dad how he had decided to make an application for Greek citizenship, but that it was a complicated process that could take years as an entitlement to dual citizenship was not automatic. I felt sad, as I knew that what I saw as a beautiful gesture of homage to my father's heritage would not come to fruition before his death.

I've always regarded my passport as one of the most important documents anyone can hold. Largely thanks to my corporate career, as well as because my husband's family lived overseas, I have travelled extensively, but to me my passport has always represented more than a little book that helps you get around the world. Its importance lies in it being part of my identity. I have always been fiercely proud of being an Australian. And no matter where I arrived in the world, I always felt a little inner pride for being the holder of an Australian passport.

The conversation lulled to a momentary silence and my brother left the room to tend to something. Suddenly, it was just me and Dad in the room. The sound of the fire crackling was punctuated by the sounds of my suppressed crying, which morphed into deep sobs. 'Dad. I am so, so sorry.' It was the first time I had broken down in front of him during his many months of illness. 'I want to do this for you too, Dad, but I just can't. I'm really proud of my Greek heritage … but I'm not Greek. I'm Australian. It just wouldn't feel right to me …'

I was mid-sentence when suddenly Dad, in his very weakened state, reached out and gave me that warm embracing hug he'd given me so many times before during my life. A hug which I realised in that moment would be one of my last from him. It made me cry more.

Through the sobs I heard Dad's whisper: 'Darling, this is our country, we all love. Our Greek heritage, we all love. I love this country. I love you and your brother. I just want you and your brother to always do what makes you happy. That's all I want. I want you both to be happy.' Dad wanted me to be happy when I felt the saddest I had ever felt in my life. We both sobbed. And then sat together and hugged each other.

My father died in 2007. After a ceremony in the Greek church, he was buried in a spot surrounded by eucalyptus trees and the sound of bellbirds. A dear friend described it to me as 'a quintessentially Australian multicultural event'.

He died many years before I even contemplated entering the world of politics. And a decade before my heritage became the subject of front-page news across the nation, with headlines such as 'Wogs out of Work' and 'The Greek Tragedy'.

This was in the midst of what became known as the citizenship crisis in Australian politics. In a wave of renewed scrutiny, many federal MPs' eligibility to sit in the parliament was put to the High Court as being in potential breach of Section 44 of Australia's constitution: the law that no member of parliament could hold citizenship of any other country than Australia.

Unlike many MPs across the parliament, I'd checked and rechecked all of this prior to signing the answer to the question as to whether I was a dual citizen. While mindful of the years of paperwork and complex bureaucracy my brother went through to become a dual citizen and the unlikelihood that I could be a Greek citizen without knowing it, the fastidious, attention-to-detail lawyer in me meant that I did my due diligence anyway.

There was never any question raised in the media about the fact that all of my immediate family (my husband and two children) are dual Australian–British citizens. But when it was leaked that my brother was a dual Greek–Australian citizen, a senior party elder rang me and yelled down the phone: 'Your bloody brother, he's a Greek. So you must be ...'

I had proudly promoted my heritage to the Greek diaspora and the microcosm of multiculturalism that made up my electorate. Early on in my election campaign I had to push to have a presence at a Greek Festival in my local community because a branch official said it wasn't important and that we shouldn't do it because it had 'never been done before'. ('Well, we've never won this seat before,' I shot back.) But this citizenship crisis incited the ready prejudice in my opponents, including many within the party to which I belonged. Zealously assisted by their friends in the right-wing media, they began fuelling a xenophobic fire.

I was absolutely not a Greek citizen. I knew there was no need for me to 'renounce' (the word *de jour* at the time). I had nothing to renounce. There was also no legal need for me to establish this with paperwork at the time – but in the context of the wild furore, I got it anyway. The written confirmation from the Greek government confirmed unequivocally that I wasn't recognised as a citizen of their country, nor was I entitled to be. To become entitled to Greek citizenship, a person had to either have their Greek parent register them in the local municipality in which they were born (which my father never did), or take proactive action to register themselves (as my brother did some ten years earlier when my father was ill, and I never did). But many people, including MPs, made the naively arrogant assumption that the laws of other non-Commonwealth countries must be the same as the law in the British countries – namely, that if a parent was born outside Australia, the entitlement to citizenship prevailed.

This whole event showed both the subtle and the overt racism that lurks in our country. The frenzied media commentary, the looks of doubt, the questions and attacks, the emergence of self-proclaimed constitutional law experts who were actually nothing more than racist media commentators and social-media trolls, the printed falsehoods, and all the political game-playing reached a crescendo of intensity. My factual message just couldn't penetrate this public storm, egged on and incited by powerful forces. Despite the support of Prime Minister Malcolm Turnbull, I felt the emotional toll of that storm's raw and brutal strength, and observed with distress how sound barriers were being put up to block out my voice.

The vicious and disturbing race-related threats often intersected with gendered abuse. One particular comment on social media is seared in my memory: 'Resign you wog criminal slut.'

At least in my local multicultural electorate, I was overwhelmed by the empathy and understanding from my constituents. They got it. They understood. They, like me, had grown up with it.

'It' was summed up in Phillip Coorey's opinion piece for the *Australian Financial Review* under the heading 'You can blame the Poms, not the wogs, for this citizenship crisis'. It explained that 'This catastrophe now engulfing the polity is not a product of politicians of non-English speaking heritage being unwittingly caught out ... This disaster ... has been inflicted by politicians almost exclusively of Anglo-Celtic stock.' The sentiment being expressed at the time reflected, a 'subconscious cultural blindness, if not arrogance.'

I remember calmly explaining to my elderly mum, who was

getting increasingly anxious about the vitriolic, racist radio and television commentary and talkback, that if I were forced to go to the High Court, it still wouldn't mean I'd done anything wrong.

I kept thinking about Dad, hugging me that day in front of the fire, when he talked of his dual love for Australia and our Greek heritage. I felt so deeply sad. As I sat in the grandeur of the House of Representatives chamber watching the dialogue and actions around the citizenship issue playing out with a gladiatorial fervour, my stomach was churning and knotted with an intense anxiety. A kind of 'job lot' of suspect dual citizens was being proposed. I remember the prime minister rhetorically asking my opponents whether they were 'seriously contending that the House should make such a fool of itself as to send off to the High Court somebody that the Greek government says is not a Greek citizen'. I looked upwards to the vast expansive ceiling and said sorry to my late dad. I was trying so hard to maintain a mask of steely stoicism, knowing all eyes (and press gallery cameras) were on me. I wasn't just sad for myself and for my family, but for all those people of migrant heritage I represented in the parliament. I just wanted to say sorry to them that this toxic sentiment had engulfed our House. And our country.

When I was alone watching the news and heard a reporter sign off his story by saying, 'Banks' father hadn't left her a legacy, rather a burden,' it felt like a knife stabbing through my Greek–Australian heart. The steely stoicism I'd diligently maintained changed – to deep visceral sobs.

I just wanted a hug from my dad.

Several months after the 'issue' had settled down, I was invited to attend a branch meeting of a career politician – a backbencher who had been elected as a government MP the same year I won the one seat in the one-seat majority. And yet, the only – literally the only – thing he said about me in his introduction was that I was an 'expert on citizenship'. Like this was my claim to fame. I recall looking at all the suspicious faces of the members in this Liberal heartland seat in Victoria and feeling as if, once again, I had to justify my existence.

The High Court has decided that federal MPs, current and future, have to live with the strict black-letter interpretation of Section 44. This is absurd for a number of reasons, but especially because, when MPs are sworn in, they pledge allegiance to the Queen – a foreign national who lives on the other side of the world.

As much as this experience felt personally violating and hurtful for me, the hurt it caused also compounded my already strong sense of responsibility as the representative of my constituents, and of all Australian people with whom I shared some form of lived experience. I became even more acutely aware of what a difference it made to my ability to represent them that I was not only a woman, but that I had a migrant working-class background and Greek heritage. The attacks on me were symbolic of the experiences that many of my constituents lived with every day. I was their voice in parliament and had a responsibility to speak up for their interests wherever and whenever I could. Because I truly knew what it was like to be one of them – and certainly knew better than the overwhelming majority of my fellow MPs – I knew how to anticipate and defend their rights at a deep and intuitive level.

In early 2019, after I had made front-page headlines in late 2018 for a speech decrying the indefinite detention of refugees, a moment of historical significance happened in our parliament: the first time in ninety years a sitting government lost a vote on its own legislation. It was a federal law supported by the crossbench MPs, including myself, that allowed asylum seekers and refugees requiring urgent medical care to be transferred from detention centres to Australia to receive that care. The Greek–Australian press reported that although my 'main legacy' was my resignation speech 'bringing to light the inherent sexism [and revealing] a culture that has long poisoned politics in Australia ... Whatever happens in Australian politics, it is all but certain that a more humane approach towards asylum seekers is in order – and that is partly due to Ms Banks' recent work.' Sadly we have not seen that humane approach eventuate.

I hoped that this work brought heart to my constituents, many of whom had been, like my father, a child refugee to this country who thrived in its warm embrace and humanity, and who are fiercely proud of their Australian citizenship.

*

It's often an emotional and gruelling dilemma as to how to deal with overt bias and discrimination when you encounter it in real time: do you ignore it, call it out, report it, walk away from it – or even laugh about it? I've generally taken the approach that personal attacks don't deserve the courtesy of a response, but when I have occasionally thought of a comeback line on the spot, I've found it's incredibly satisfying. It is even satisfying to think of what you *could* have said.

Above all, seeking the support of those you love and trust is the crucial element to getting through. Being resilient to attacks doesn't mean having to suck it up and deal with it alone – and that's particularly true during a crisis, even if it's your own personal crisis. In any situation, whether you're at school, in the workplace, a senior leader in your field or a public figure, the best solace can be found in surrounding yourself with people who love you, colleagues who you trust, people who make you laugh and feel happy. And people who give you hugs.

But beyond combatting and coping with prejudice at a personal level, it is of critical importance that our leaders, in politics, business and beyond, take an active role in stamping out prejudice and supporting those who have to deal with it. The best leaders in business are the ones who live and breathe inclusivity – who recognise their own biases, and who hold those to account who don't do the same. The leaders who listen, who have the intellect and empathy to understand in this context, and who provide you support are second to none.

I don't believe it's a coincidence that emboldened racism and cultural prejudice came out in Australian politics during that period in 2017 when, less than a year earlier, Donald Trump was elected president. US politics under Trump was characterised by sexism, racism and bigotry – elements of which have undoubtedly come across the ocean to our shores. Right-wing forces in my state even started promoting the slogan 'Make Victoria Great Again'.

We are now lucky to have seen Kamala Harris make history, and it is significant that she is described in official Democratic literature as a 'Black and Asian American woman'. It's comforting, to say the least, that, as Anne Summers wrote for the *Sydney Morning Herald*, 'Biden and Harris represent an utter repudiation of the Trump era.'

It's important to take confidence in the fact that millions of people of non-English speaking heritage – not just the US Vice-President and other notable people, but people of all walks of life – have dealt with prejudice and discrimination throughout their lives in their own way, and still have successfully carved their own path towards leadership positions.

In Australia, the unacknowledged violence in our history hinders much of what we could do towards reconciliation. I fundamentally believe that careful listening and education are among the best tools for a more unified country. Changing the date of Australia Day, constitutional recognition of Indigenous sovereignty, and Australia becoming a republic are all examples of things that could be done for a more reconciled and harmonious Australia.

Remembering our history and conserving our traditions is important for us all – no matter in which stage of Australian history our ancestry resides. But listening to each other's stories about what has created division in the past and making structural changes to ensure redress and reconciliation will mean that future generations can look back proudly on our history. I believe our intransigence when it comes to change so far has been because most of the people in power only have the lived experience of those same people who have historically been in power. Diversity in leadership is integral to ensuring that a true and full understanding of our history and our present informs the decisions that are made, so that we inhabit a country that includes and values all of us. Where we don't yet have diversity in leadership, the next best thing is a leader who truly respects all people.

From our distance across the Tasman, I know I'm not the only Australian who has long admired the way in which New Zealand, unlike Australia, has established what has been described as a 'comfortable biculturalism' with their Indigenous population. Laura Tingle asks of us in Australia when it comes to our First Nations people: 'Maori culture is increasingly seen as New Zealand's culture … Why is it so much harder for us to embrace this extraordinary, ancient culture, let alone acknowledge the hard legal realities that our courts have recognised in our history?'

How the actions and words of leaders make people feel counts. Leaders with a public profile say and do many things that are hurtful, discriminatory and prejudiced against people from minority groups. Indigenous or culturally and linguistically diverse people, the LGBTQIA+ community and people living with disability, invisible or otherwise, are often treated with a lack of humanity. People never forget how you make them feel.

I can only begin to imagine how people felt across Australia when a senator invoked the 'final solution' and the White Australia policy in his maiden speech. At least by the next day the parliament had united, and speeches were made by MPs across the party divide, including myself. Phillip Coorey wrote that people like me and Anne Aly broke down in parliament that day while speaking 'as they felt the need to justify their existence because their heritage excluded them from [the senator's] view of Australia', and that was exactly how it was. It was one of the saddest times for me in the parliament.

Unexpectedly, one of my happiest times in parliament happened around the same time as the Section 44 citizenship pressure: it was in that same period that the marriage equality legislation was passed. The process and the plebiscite were not the favoured way and caused much angst for the LGBTQIA+ community, but the outcome achieved may not have otherwise been reached for years. The same people in my party who fuelled the citizenship suspicions against me were those who were vehemently opposed to my advocacy for the 'Yes' vote. I was one of only seven MPs who became known as the '100 percenters', as we voted for the marriage equality legislation without any amendment, and my opinion piece in support was published in both the mainstream and Greek–Australian media. My multicultural electorate supported the 'Yes' vote in the same majority numbers as the national vote.

Just before the legislation passed, I was in a one-on-one meeting with Malcolm Turnbull about the citizenship situation. I remember appreciating his leadership in this time: his wise counsel and calm in the citizenship storm, and his extraordinary respect for all people. This respect undoubtedly played a role in clearing the path to marriage equality, despite the resistance in his party.

About an hour after our meeting we were in the chamber, the 'people's house', and the power of the people won. Turnbull proudly declared, 'We've voted today for equality, for love.' My anxiety over the citizenship crisis melted away as people broke into song, together voicing the words 'We are Australian'. (Perhaps the Seekers song could be our new national anthem when we become a republic?) MPs from across the floor of the House of Representatives and people in the public gallery, people in the streets, people watching it on their televisions in pubs and at home – it felt as if the whole country had stopped to share this great moment in Australian history. A victory for equality. For unity. For mutual respect. For all Australians.

It was a moment I will always treasure. By focusing on increasing diversity in leadership in all spheres, and basing our actions and words on respect for all people, my fervent hope is that we will see many more moments like this one.

Chapter 5

Having your all

'Women can have it all, but not all at the same time.'

This was famously said by Madeleine Albright (who explained she began to focus on her career only after her divorce from her marriage of twenty-two years that had produced three children). It was of course in answer to what was dubbed the question of our time: 'Can women have it all?' It's often asked with a kind of wise-oracle tone – usually at business forums when talking about working mothers.

Upon my telling her that I was pregnant, a female executive director, about fifteen years my senior, said, 'Wow that's great. See, nowadays you can have a career *and* kids. *You can have it all.* In my day, I had to make a conscious decision to sacrifice having children.'

Does this mean your 'all' must include children? And why doesn't this question of having it all apply to men, too? Is that because we are meant to assume that men have had *it all* for centuries?

'It all' should be changed to 'your all' – the 'all' that defines your own unique aspirations for a fulfilling life, separate from what convention says you should want.

Whatever it is, though, your all must coexist with other responsibilities and can be affected weekly, daily, annually or through the decades by life events: falling in love, breaking up, divorce, the death of a loved one, a new job opportunity, loss of employment, serious illness, a holiday or sabbatical – events that are both within and outside your control. These deeply human events can affect your all at any time, regardless of whether you have children, don't have children, are single, married, or have a partner or others to care for, such as elderly parents.

Unfortunately, statistics and research confirm that, as women continue to encounter gender-stereotyped judgement and questions about the choices they make, most of these care roles do indeed fall disproportionately on women.

Ada Calhoun describes the struggle for the women born between 1965 and 1980: Generation X 'are experiencing a different middle age than our mothers and grandmothers did. As a generation, X is small, a great baby bust, and we are now caring for the far larger generations that tower over us on either side – often while working full-time.'

Having your all is a kind of perpetual aspirational state, only made genuinely achievable by an independence that enables you to make your own decisions. No matter how much or how little you consult with friends and family, no matter the judgement and questions, no matter the societal, financial, workplace and political expectations or limitations, no matter the curve balls life may throw at you, if you have that independence, you can be within reach of your all.

But there is no question that gender stereotyping can stymie you having your all if you let it – or if you impose unreasonable expectations on yourself.

*

Pregnancy, childbirth and parenthood are a big curve ball of life. As are other experiences: abortion, miscarriage, the trials and tribulations of IVF, stillbirth, postnatal depression, endometriosis, gynaecological cancers – to name a few. All of these events hugely impact people's lives and their expectations of themselves.

I will never forget a female executive who insisted on returning to the workforce full-time after having her first child. In that insistence, she kept denying that she had serious postnatal depression. With support, she eventually found the courage to admit she needed help, and when she recovered, she generously shared the understanding she had gained with others. What she had found important to her recovery was knowing that after the birth of your baby, it's okay to just learn and accept – that you don't have to be in constant pursuit of being 'the mother I dreamed I would be'.

For a lot of successful businesspeople, parenting can come into conflict with your primary skill set. For example, planning. One of my friends is a meticulous planner and, after ten years of practising in the legal profession, had her firstborn soon after I had mine. In her desperately fatigued postnatal haze, she said to me, 'I wish you'd told me what it was like. I would have just bought another dog.' She added, pointing to her beautiful newborn daughter, 'At least I could plan my day before I had this.' My friend and I laugh about it now, but it's a stark reminder that sometimes black humour is the best way to express your feelings. (My friend's daughter is much loved and so is her son. And she's always loved dogs.)

For many women who've enjoyed a career and throw pregnancy and parenthood into the mix, no single description for the challenge they face – be that 'managing the juggle', the mummy wars, the sexism, the workplace inflexibility, the guilt – will necessarily be the right one. It's too complex and too personal. Situations may arise that are unique to you and you alone.

There is only seventeen months in age difference between my two children. 'Two kids under two wasn't in the plan,' I always said to people.

And one particular day during my second pregnancy especially wasn't in the plan.

It so happened that new parenthood coupled with working at a demanding job coincided with my husband having an equally demanding job and a significant travel schedule. He was away for 40 per cent of the year. The unpaid workload fell more 'generously' on me. I used to say it was like being 'a single mum without the sympathy'. This somehow kept my spirits up.

It was just another weekday, but my anxiety levels were high. Extremely high. My husband was already at the office and going straight from there to Singapore for yet another business trip. My toddler son was sick, now on antibiotics, but still not well enough to go to creche. I was feeling unwell, too – but for a different reason. I had morning sickness, which had been affecting me throughout most of my second pregnancy – now at the twenty-four-week mark.

I was watching my son sleep – we had both been awake most of the night. *Children look so blissful when they're asleep*, I thought, bursting with love and emotion through my fatigued, unwell haze. Then I snapped back to practical thought. The carer was late. 'Sorry, *traffic*,' said her cryptic text. This didn't help my anxiety levels. I would be late – extremely late – for an important all-day board meeting.

Miraculously, forty-five minutes later, I arrived at the office. This had required a form of multitasking that was, on reflection, extremely dangerous: applying makeup while scoffing a muesli bar for breakfast, participating in a conference call and driving. The meeting was well underway. When I proffered my apology (which didn't contain all the 'child is sick, carer late' details), the frosty silence from my colleagues around the table echoed back at me jarringly.

The meeting proceeded. A product that represented a significant proportion of the company's profit had been recalled and had now been off the shelf for five months. We were in the middle of an intense debate on our strategic plan for the relaunch, and I was playing a critical part.

I was so engrossed in the discussion that I was barely aware of my first contraction. At the third contraction, I realised and dismissed it as a 'Braxton Hicks' (a false labour). Then there was another. And twelve minutes later, another. By this time, I was looking at my watch. Ten minutes later, another.

I looked around the room and was suddenly hit by an acute awareness that I couldn't trust how any of my colleagues, all men, would react. My intuition led me to decide not to share the details of what was going on with my body. I quietly left the room under the guise of yet another loo break. (My colleagues had become used to me going in and out of these meetings, as the scheduled breaks weren't frequent enough for my pregnancy-induced requirements.)

I walked straight to my office, closed the door, rang my doctor, and started off by saying, 'It's probably nothing, probably Braxton Hicks, but ... they're regular. Every ten to fifteen minutes or so.'

In the middle of my self-diagnosis rant, my obstetrician said, in a concerned but controlled tone, 'Julia. Get an ambulance.

Get yourself to the Royal Women's Hospital. I'll meet you there in fifteen minutes.'

An ambulance would cause too much fuss – and probably take longer than a taxi, I reasoned. The only person I told was my EA, with strict instructions not to say anything.

In the taxi, all I could think was 'Twenty-four weeks is too early. The baby will die.'

I was rushed into the emergency ward, and there was the reassuring presence of my obstetrician and his team, among the heart monitors, wires tubes, nursing staff everywhere, questions, forms to fill in and people talking to me. 'We'll ring your husband … He shouldn't go to Singapore.'

And then, what had been looking very much like a medical emergency suddenly and mercifully seemed to stop.

'Baby has decided it's too early to come out,' they told me. 'Baby's fine.'

Only then did I start crying.

Still lying in the hospital emergency ward, but recovering from the trauma of it all, my thoughts went back to work. I rang one of the directors, not the CEO. Before I could say anything, he bellowed down the phone, 'Where the hell are you?' It was obvious he was still irritated by my earlier tardiness.

I explained my predicament: baby was in danger, possible premature labour, had to sneak out, didn't want to cause a fuss, son sick, husband overseas, emergency ward, hospital …

His impatience got the better of him and he interrupted: 'Yeah, yeah, okay, so will you be in tomorrow?'

'It depends,' I said, stunned.

'On what?'

'On whether I have a baby or not.'

The nurse tending to me, overhearing the conversation,

did a comforting eye-roll as she continued to take my blood pressure.

The director did apologise to me for his outburst. But when I described this incident to people, I didn't anticipate the fully loaded questions I would receive in response. Under the guise of concern was always the hint of being judged. 'With your husband having such a high-travel job, how do you manage it?' And: 'How *could* you do it? A sick child at home, too?' The worst was: 'Do you think the stress of your job is what brought this on? Should you reconsider?'

Oh, the questions. During pregnancy and motherhood, your equilibrium is often punctured by the things people say, and especially by the questions they ask. The words seem harmless, but are loaded. As Annabel Crabb describes at length in *The Wife Drought*, there is a traditional model of the woman at home or in part-time work and the man as the main breadwinner working long hours. If you don't fit this model, the norm – or the norm as people believe it to be – you will come under intense pressure to conform to it.

My second baby went to full term, and after a short period of maternity leave, I planned my return to work. On my first day back, resettling into my office, I got a familiar feeling. That same tormented emotional tug that I had often experienced after my first stint of maternity leave when driving to or arriving at the office. It was the feeling of wanting to be in two places at the same time: at home with my baby and at work.

My thoughts were interrupted by a knock on my office door. A friendly male colleague said warmly, 'Hi Julia. Welcome back. Got a minute?' We proceeded to have one of those happy collegial chats about the joys and trials of new parenthood. About six months prior, he and his wife had celebrated the birth of their second child and we got into comparing notes and sharing photos.

Then he said, 'Yes, my wife, she's not like you ... she *really* loves the children.' My face must have started contorting at that point, because he looked like he realised he'd said the wrong thing. He quickly pressed on, talking nervously without taking in air. And made it worse.

When I finally responded, it was partly in anger, part defensive and part joking. 'Oh ... what about you then? Don't you *really* love your children? What are you doing back at work?'

Sure enough, he blustered that he didn't mean it that way.

It's not just the women with children who face questions and judgement. During their childbearing years (which, thanks to modern medicine, are now extended), the questions still come readily for women without children, with a stunning overlay of oblivion and insensitivity to the multitude of complex reasons as to why or why not a woman might be a mother. Women in leadership are still judged through the lens of whether they have children or not. If they have children, the judgement is often that, by continuing in full-time work, they're being neglectful of their child, shameless, selfish or missing out on precious experiences. If they don't have children, they're often treated with suspicion or pity, even if they are unable to or choose not to have children.

*

One of my best default mechanisms to deal with questions or judgement is humour. It's especially satisfying when you can rely on a particular third party to provide the humour – the kids themselves. Though at other times they break your heart. There's nothing like your own children to stir up the whole gamut of emotions relating to the strain of balancing work and family with one little move or comment. Whether it makes you laugh, cry, feel sad or happy, these little cherubs cut through to the truth of what you're feeling.

One cold and wintry day we were all stuck inside. The familiar deep, relentless fatigue and overwhelming exhaustion of juggling work and family and everything else had set in with a vengeance. It was worsened by jet lag and the weather. My toddlers were playing with Lego in front of me, and I was trying to concentrate on 'being present' – adhering to the advice of all the leadership wellbeing texts.

Suddenly I was jolted out of a deep slumber. Two little brown button eyes were centimetres from my face. A very loud but friendly child's voice rang in my ears: 'Mummy, don't go to sleep. It's just like when you're away.' (Sad.)

It was right up there with the moment when my toddler clung to my leg screaming 'Don't leave me' as I got in the taxi headed for the airport to go on another business trip. (Cry.)

Once, our nanny and I demonstrated extraordinary teamwork as we frantically tore the living area of my house apart. I had to get to the office for an important deal negotiation meeting, and we were looking for my lost car keys with the kind of crazy fervour that would have surpassed that of the most enthusiastic home burglars.

My toddler's little squeaky voice got our attention. Until then, we had been totally oblivious to him. He looked so sweet, seated in the corner of the room with his blanky, peacefully watching the 'Nanny and Mummy show'. 'Mummy keys gone. Mummy no work,' he said, eyes twinkling. He had worked out that when I took my car keys, that meant absences from home. Negotiating with him for the location of said car keys was far more stressful than the deal I was about to negotiate. (Sad cry, happy laugh.)

My children grew up only ever knowing that both their parents worked, and so they didn't think anything of it. But there was a mum at my child's preschool who liked to shoot the occasional 'joking' barb my way for working full-time with 'such a ridiculous travel schedule'. Or she would sing out 'I don't know how she does it' – a phrase that was already a cliché before the book and movie.

My four-year-old son had been selected to play the part of Joseph in the school Christmas play. A group of amazing women at the school, including my friends, had volunteered to take on the task of making the costumes. One of these women, however, was that regular critic of my working life.

During the weeks in the lead-up to the performance, I had to go on a business trip to New York and, as my husband was caught up at work, my friend, also a volunteer costume maker, had kindly helped out even more by doing the after-care pick-up. My critic was doing the fittings of my son's costume and my friend overheard the conversation.

'Where's your mummy this time?'

'Oh, she's in New somewhere.'

'New somewhere?'

'Yes. It's either New York or New Zealand.'

'Well, when your mummy comes back from wherever she is, maybe she can sew up the rest of your costume so it doesn't fall off you in the middle of the play.'

I was always genuinely grateful for the volunteer work of school parents during business hours, and strived my best to also volunteer where I could on weekends and after hours. But when my critic said this to my son, my protective friend felt this message was clearly meant for me and translated as a taunt to my son. She was about to interrupt to go to his rescue, but she didn't need to. The comment was lost on him.

'Oh, my mummy doesn't *sew*. She *works*.' (Laugh.)

I've told that story a few times. At women's business leadership forums, it's warmly received, with laughter and nods of collective agreement. But not so much when I've taken that story outside the 'target audience'.

Once, as an MP I shared this story on daytime national television during an interview about working women. The negative responses, by phone and social media, came in thick and fast and stunned me. Many of them contained vile gendered abuse around me not staying home and being a 'proper mother'. One man called me 'a disgusting excuse for a mother'.

These deeply entrenched assumptions can reveal themselves to career women in any industry or sector, but my time in politics showed me that gender stereotypical norms are ever present in that sphere, and that having a public profile invites and emboldens people to openly express their bias towards you.

*

'Redundant.' I'd been in the meeting for about half an hour, and that was the only word that I could hear.

'It's important that you know that your role is redundant, not you,' said the HR director, intending to comfort me. I just kept hearing 'redundant'. Redundant at a company that I'd worked with for sixteen years – the majority of my corporate career – while juggling the life of raising two children. Nonetheless, I was excited about the prospect of new beginnings.

I started looking for work almost straight away. Considering our family life and juggle, I began contemplating going part-time.

But then, soon after, my husband came home one evening and announced he'd been offered another job which meant an even more intense overseas travel job, or the alternative of a redundancy package. He took the redundancy.

My son, now in primary school, said, 'Does that mean I've got two unemployed parents?'

We shared the story of my son's question with a group at a drinks function, where the response was all laughter and fun, given these people had probably done their own calculations about the financial outcomes for such long-serving high-paid employees. But they also knew we were both too young to retire. When the conversation turned to our future employment plans, my husband was queried at length. All eyes were on him. There was a lull, and then someone in the group turned to me and said, 'At least now you can stay home, look after the kids, and reacquaint yourself with them after all these years of working.'

A job means money and power. For men and women. And so it's a concern when women say, and really believe, that their husband's job is more important than their own.

It wasn't long before my husband landed a job that meant him working from home in a role that was far less demanding than his previous high-flying executive role, and that allowed him to be around more with the kids. Meanwhile, I secured a full-time senior executive role that had all the same demands of my previous job, and then some, including extensive overseas and interstate travel.

In the period before I secured my new job, I used my new-found freedom to do, among other things, the school pick-up. I was making small talk with a fully-fledged stay-at-home mum, who'd always extolled the virtues of her way of life in a way I found irritating. Saved by the bell, my mobile rang. I took a call from a recruiter, and when I came back, I explained to her that I was excited because a new job was in the pipeline.

'Oh, for goodness's sake. Why get back into work again so quickly. Why not stay home and catch up on all the things you missed out on with your children?'

'We haven't missed out on anything with our children,' I replied without hesitation. I was genuinely confused that she would think that. And I remember surprising myself by saying 'we'. '*We* haven't missed out on anything with our children.'

'We just made it work' is the often-quoted statement of a dual-working couple. It makes it all sound so simple, seamless and sunny. But for most couples it's more often complicated, chaotic and difficult. An imperfect balance, while trying to have 'your all'.

We have been a dual career couple throughout our children's lives. We both had demanding jobs that required travel and home absences, and my husband and I figured out how to live our lives so that when there was conflict, neither of our careers were treated as second-best. If we had a clash, we'd make a quick determination of what was more important and how one or the other could manoeuvre around it. There were peaks and troughs in terms of high-priority matters for each of our careers. And then we had the benefit of help from my parents, particularly my mum, when there were clashes of priority.

School and sport drop-offs, laundry and general household management all pretty much got done. But it was all very clumsy, clunky and chaotic.

We basically picked up the chores that 'went to our strengths'. Food and cooking have a special place for me – they're one of my greatest joys and hobbies. I see cooking for my family and friends as an expression of my love for them. And of all the activities I enjoyed doing with my kids, cooking was perhaps my favourite. Not only did I get to do something I loved with the little people I love most in the world, it also meant they were always well fed.

But despite cooking not being one of my husband's strengths, the kids were still well fed even when I was away. Once on a business trip, I called home and my heart warmed as it always did when one of my children answered the phone.

'What did you have for dinner tonight?'

'Pizza in the box,' said my son.

'And last night?'

'Indian takeaway.'

'And on Monday, when Mummy first left?'

'Thai from the nice shop in High Street.'

'Okay sweetie, that's great … can you please put Daddy on the phone?'

I think that's the reason my children were never ever fussy eaters.

The cliché of work-life balance was unattainable. It was a life full of imperfect balance – constantly correcting this way and that to stay upright. Any other way would have meant our careers wouldn't have taken the paths they did. But together, we managed.

'If she wants children and a job, a woman's life is only as good as the man or woman she marries. That's the biggest unspoken truth I know. All too often, women marry their glass ceilings.' So says feminist Caitlin Moran, and in my own life and observing the lives of the women around me, I have found it to be true again and again. I could not have had 'my all' without the support of my husband. And if your partner believes, overtly or unconsciously, in the biases and judgements that block women's careers, you will, as Moran says, have married your own glass ceiling.

In my maiden speech to parliament in 2016 I said, 'The glass ceiling … cannot simply be broken by women alone. Rather, it can only be lifted out, removed and taken away by men and women together, so that our businesses, parliaments and our communities are representative of the diversity of our great people.'

I said 'we' at that school gate conversation because my husband was never my glass ceiling. I said 'we' because there is no way I would have been able to accomplish in my career without him. I said 'we' because I innately knew that my husband believed that my success was as important to him as his own success. And vice versa. And I knew that 'success' for both of us meant being happy in our work and raising children who knew they were loved. And well fed.

*

The research is unequivocal that in Australia and around the world, women do more unpaid work than their male partners. No matter the stage of their career, no matter whether both partners are in the paid workforce full-time, and no matter whether they have children or not. Meanwhile, the fact remains that on average women earn 18 per cent less than men, and there is a 40 per cent retirement gap in savings.

The emergence of flexible, remote and part-time work has been a double-edged sword. While it has helped women stay in the paid workforce when they start a family, it has been at a cost to their career trajectory and earning power. A paper from 2016 shows that 'working part-time includes a reduction in promotion opportunities. Part-time roles do not offer the same security and predictability as full-time roles, often carry less responsibility and can mean limited career options.'

Structural and governance consequences from the COVID-19 pandemic have exposed some glaring gaps – for every person, of every age, of every socio-economic demographic. These included gaps in mental health support for single people and those who live alone – both young and old – as well as the gap in the disproportionate amount of unpaid work women do compared to their male counterparts, including child care and elder care, domestic labour, home-schooling, all in addition to the extra so-called mental load they normally carry. But the pandemic has shown that flexible and remote work can happen, and shouldn't just be considered a practical perk for mums or parents with kids.

Even before the pandemic, many organisations in many sectors implemented huge changes to support a flexible workplace culture. In the world of federal politics, there are many aspects that make the workplace very palatable for working parents – and indeed in better ways than most other organisations. There are plenty of examples where female MPs clearly share caring responsibilities and prove they can be 'female' and an 'MP' all at the same time.

Being a federal MP is not the only job in the world that demands long hours, night-time conference calls, overnight absences and travel, and the parliament provides structures that aren't available to a lot of people in other professions. There is onsite child care and, uniquely, a carer or family member may accompany you to work. Though there is still room for improvement: for example, they could not have sitting hours until eight at night, introduce more remote working or even remote voting, and substitute a portion of sitting weeks to enable MPs to do more work in their electorates.

After fifteen successful years as a federal MP, Kate Ellis stepped down from politics following the birth of her second child, knowing that people would say that politics must not be compatible with motherhood. But she also later observed, 'How lucky was I that I had a newborn child, I had a job that I absolutely loved that was stimulating and rewarding, and I got to travel with my child, I got to take my child to work with me … There's not many jobs out there that mothers can do that.'

But although more and more workplaces have already embraced flexible work practices, it's important not to assume, let alone say, 'it's easier than it was in my day'. It may well not be. These increased choices may in fact make it harder for women in some cases. And the gender stereotyping remains. Many of us, myself included, have seen men praised for leaving the meeting early to go to a parent-teacher interview, in the same organisations where if a woman left the office early to do pick-up, she was considered to be taking the 'walk of shame'.

At the National Press Club, a few days before my maiden speech in parliament, former Prime Minister John Howard said, 'I'm not sure that you will ever have a fifty/fifty thing because it's a fact of society that the caring role, whatever people may say about it and whatever the causes are … women play a significantly greater part of filling the caring role in our communities, which inevitably will place some limits on their capacity.' For good measure he added, 'Some people may say: "What a terrible thing to say" … it just happens to be the truth.'

I couldn't let this go through to the keeper. I added the following paragraph to my maiden speech: 'It is never right to say never. It is true to say that women have borne the brunt of caring responsibilities, but it is not right to say that we will never achieve a fifty/fifty ratio, simply because that has been the case historically. This is the modern world.'

No organisation can spin-doctor its way out of gender inequality in the workplace. There needs to be substantive structural change at a macro political level. That said – don't underestimate your personal power to help make those structural changes.

A few years after my premature birth scare, sitting around that same boardroom table, I was part of a very robust and animated debate about paid maternity leave. Twelve months unpaid leave, giving up your car and suspending super was the standard entitlement for executives at my level back then. An HR guy who was junior to me even suggested that my corporate paid health insurance should be cancelled, saying, 'You're not sick, you're just having a baby.'

I strongly advocated for paid maternity leave and a month's salary as a return-to-work bonus. One would think that my status not only as the only woman but as the only mother on the board at that time might have magnified my voice and influence on that board decision. But during the break, one director quietly took me aside and asked, 'Are you just so strong on this because you're intending to have your third child?' We had only ever intended to have two children, and the idea that I would be fighting so hard just for my own benefit rather than for that of other women coming after me seemed to me to demonstrate the small-minded way in which this man thought about people's motivations – and failed to think himself of the possibilities for improving equality in the workplace. Fortunately, his view was in the minority and, despite the robust debate, the new policy was implemented.

There's no doubt that workplace culture and the leadership and managerial qualities of your direct boss are both critical elements to the success of any leadership journey: it's important to have a leader or manager who supports you as the person you are and not just as an employee. This includes understanding what else you are balancing – whether that's parental or elder care, or care for a family member or friend with a disability, care for foster children that involves transitory arrangements and responsibilities, or volunteer work that may overlap in work life.

In the private practice and corporate world there are some inspiring examples of women (and some men) who have been promoted to partner, director and senior roles while working through a part-time role. These instances could not have happened without the support of those in power – who are more often than not men. However, these examples are often counterbalanced by ones where there is a decided lack of support.

It is secret women's business, but when I'm talking among my female friends about difficulties with a male boss, the question we always pose to each other is, 'Does his wife work?' We usually know the answer. We know if a male boss has a working wife, he is invariably a better boss.

Once, a female lawyer and single mum, who worked in one of the big six firms, confided in me at a conference. She had a full-time role with demanding twelve-hour days, and had asked her traditionalist senior male partner boss if she could work from home for two of her days. He told her that she could, but that she'd never make partner because she wouldn't be *seen* at the office as much, and because people and the clients may 'get wind of the fact' that she was 'looking after the kids between phone calls'.

At the opposite end of the spectrum was my was one of my 'dotted line' bosses, a senior VP. Once at about 11 pm, my husband was told it was urgent that he get on an early flight to Sydney the next morning. This clashed with our plans for him to do the school drop-off so that I could attend a high-pressure budget review with our parent company's VIP executives, who had flown in from overseas. I sent a grovelling email to my boss at 11.30 pm explaining that I would be a half hour late. He was still up, rehearsing the presentation, and pinged back straight away: 'No worries Julia. Don't stress. See you there.'

Okay. Breathe. Such a feeling of relief.

At the end of the next day, my boss came over and praised me for my presentation. But the best bit was when he said, 'Oh and by the way, that email you sent me last night: you *never* have to apologise or worry about that stuff. I know you work. I know you're diligent. You're great. Never stress about that.'

In my mind, he went straight to the category of one of the best bosses I'd ever had.

Once I was in the audience at a massive corporate luncheon event for International Women's Day. There were at least six hundred guests, mainly women. After the speeches, which were all by high-flying corporate female leaders, there was a Q and A session. One woman raised her hand, noted she had just been promoted and indicated that her aspiration was ultimately to be like the international corporate leader sitting on the panel. Her question was around how, with her new promotion, she had to participate in late-night conference calls with the parent company bosses – the people she aspired to being one day. She was struggling with this because of how it affected her personal life, and she wanted to 'get more work-life balance'. I remember thinking to myself that if you worked for a global organisation headquartered in a different hemisphere, as I had done throughout my corporate career, work in different timezones came with the territory. I'm sure that every woman in that room, including the panel members, could have told her what they themselves would do, but that only she could decide what *she* could do.

My 'all' is being surrounded by my family and friends, and having financial security and independence. I've always struggled with work-life balance as a concept, let alone as a reality. This image of two separate things on a kind of balancing scale that you calmly weigh out and line up doesn't equate with my experience of life. Rather, I've always seen work and life integrated, with an overlay of love – and more than a touch of chaotic mess.

Whatever the situation in your personal or private life, and no matter whether you have children or not, for most of us, work is a significant, meaningful and important part of our lives. The way life – real life – actually works is that sometimes work has to take priority and sometimes outside interests or obligations have to take priority. It will rarely be that you are able to make choices you're 100 per cent happy with at all times, but in the end it always has to be your choice. You alone can make the call – case by case.

But as much as these decisions are personal and it's up to you to navigate what is more important to you in the instances where work and outside life compete, it does make an enormous difference to have a supportive employer.

The 2020 pandemic has changed the workplace dynamic by proving that flexible integration, rather than separation, of work and life can mean that the job will still get done. The key now is for responsible and accountable leadership teams to address the difficulties thrown up by this new way of working, so that they don't waste the opportunities that come with it. It's important that all structures and organisations use the pandemic as a trigger to improve their workplace culture – and they can start by looking through the gender lens.

In this past year, we have seen kids in the background of zoom calls, heard dogs barking, and been more closely exposed to how each of our colleagues manages the juggle. The lockdowns also taught us that loneliness is not just something that afflicts the elderly. Good organisations and corporations around the country have been very deliberate about ensuring that occupational health and safety includes mental health support. The upside of the 2020 pandemic is that it has forced many organisations who've resisted it until now to rethink their values and policies (such as working from home) in relation to their most important asset: their employees.

Leadership is hard. And often lonely. But behind every great leader is a great network of loved ones. That applies whether a leader is male or female, single or in a relationship, with or without kids. Support from friends, family and community helps people to be better in the workplace. In turn, workplaces need to support people to be better friends, family and community members. That's life. That's work. And that's fine, as long as you feel satisfied that 'having your all' is your biggest and most important work in progress.

Chapter 6

The only woman in the room

The only woman around the board table. The only woman on the executive team. The only woman at the meeting.

This is a scene which has lessened over the years, but still happens in the rooms off the corridors of power.

I recall one particular meeting in which I was the only woman in the room. It was in a backbencher MP's office in Parliament House: our first meeting of the newly formed House of Representatives Economics Committee. I was sitting in between two other MPs on the standard-issue couch.

The plan had been to institutionalise regular accountability for the banks through the committee's Banking Inquiry, and this meeting was just prior to the scheduled public hearing, in which the appointed MPs (from across party lines) would question and cross examine the CEOs of the big four banks.

It was a big deal. The mainstream media were going to be there with bells on, and so were the public, including many customers who'd had horrendous issues and experiences with the banks. There was also to be interrogation about some of the more recent bank scandals, which included workplace misconduct and misogynistic behaviour.

As the six government MP representatives on the committee, we were planning the structure of the hearing and who would ask what questions. It was agreed that, given my extensive corporate experience, which none of the others had, I would cover governance and workplace culture issues.

When the meeting concluded, we had only a few minutes remaining to walk to the public hearing. At that moment, one of the MPs I was seated next to went to stand up and placed his hand on my bare knee (I was wearing a skirt) as if to steady himself for a second. Then he got to his feet, took a deep breath and said with the authoritative tone of an expert in the field (which he was not), 'Look, guys, the plan's all good except for one thing. I think I should do Julia's line of questioning.'

As he said this, he avoided looking at me and instead looked around at all the blokes in the room, as if soliciting their consent. I stared at him quizzically (while still slightly taken aback by the bare-skin contact), determined to force him to meet my eye. 'Why?' I asked.

'Oh because … I think if you ask those questions it will be a bit too "burn the bra" aggressive-ish?'

The whole room was silent. One guy was staring at the carpet of his office, looking as stunned as I was. Another was nodding in earnest agreement, as if his male colleague had identified a key insight.

I maintained my stare and stoicism and said, 'Thanks … but I've got this.' The nodder stopped nodding, looking stunned at my firm tone.

As a group we walked towards the public hearing room's back

entrance, which was restricted to MPs and staffers. Security was tight. All the male MPs were striding ahead of me, talking loudly, magnifying their presence. They swept authoritatively past the security guards with an air of entitlement and filed in one after the other.

As I approached the door only seconds after them, the security guard took slow deliberate steps to block the entrance, looking at me the whole time, and then raised his hand up. 'Excuse me, Ma'am, your ID pass?' he said, signalling that he expected me to be wearing a highly visible lanyard – which is what the staffers wear. The MPs all wear a small green lapel pin.

I pointed to my pin and walked past the now red-faced security guard. I am told the security guards at Parliament House are so highly trained that they should know and recognise MPs' faces – but at the very least they should look at the lapel pin. I guess this security guard was so used to seeing only male MPs with lapel pins. It was just a mistake, but his timing was terrible.

The enquiry proceeded well and there was praise, particularly directly from the corporate community, for my robust questioning underpinned by my business knowledge. A headline in the *Australian Financial Review* read 'How Julia Banks made [ANZ CEO] Shayne Elliott squirm'.

It gradually became clear to me that the male MPs wanted to ask the tough questions not because it would be less 'burn the bra', but more because they wanted their name in print.

I just wanted to do my job.

A number of people noticed I was the only woman on the committee – including the opposition party, who swiftly substituted one of their MPs with a female MP. Despite their higher numbers of women MPs, perhaps they too initially shared the bias that this inquiry was for 'the big boys'.

Indeed, one of the opposition MPs took petty casual sexism to a new level when, at a subsequent session of the hearing, he tweeted a photo of a skeleton saying that depicted how he felt 'waiting for Julia Banks MP the point of to get to her question'. Posting on social media *during* a formal and public proceeding criticising the skills of your colleague (albeit on the other side of politics) is inappropriate and arguably in breach of the protocols, but above all I could not help thinking how different it would be if a woman displayed that kind of infantile behaviour.

Leaving aside that tweet, I was receiving enough pushback from my own side of the room as it was. As I concluded my questioning session of the next CEO, the MP sitting next to me said in a faux-mock tone, 'Phwoar! I wouldn't want to be on the wrong side of you.'

The irony of what played out during those hearings was palpable to me. My questions were directed to the immensely powerful male CEOs of the big four banks about their lack of workplace governance and their blokey cultures. I was doing that, for the most part, as the only woman in the room, beside other powerful men. Unlike most of those men, I had years of extensive experience in the governance and corporate sectors, and yet I had to validate my entitlement to ask the questions, and even to get through security. Meanwhile, some of the male MPs anointed to interrogate the CEOs about their workplace cultures were engaging in the same blokey behaviour themselves. Some of them in real time before and during those very hearings.

At the leadership end of many businesses and industries, and in politics at all levels of government, these scenarios that reinforce sexism and discrimination are played out again and again – though often in subtler and more covert ways than they did at those hearings. In some workplace cultures, the acceptance of misogyny and the patterns of behaviour that form around it are so entrenched that many of those in power are blind to these games.

It's been proven time and again that appointing women to senior leadership positions will mean increased profitability for the companies that do it. The links between female leadership, productivity and profitability are solid and proven. The combined research of the Australian Workplace Gender Equality Agency and Bankwest Curtin Economics Centre found that there is a 4.9 per cent increase in company market value for those ASX-listed entities that achieve an increase of ten percentage points or more in terms of the number of women on their boards. Appointing a female CEO has resulted in a 5 per cent increase in market value for those ASX-listed companies that have done so. Gender equal leadership teams pay – not just in terms of profitability, but also in creating healthy workplace reforms and policy outcomes.

Decisions made by gender-equal leadership teams will necessarily result in better policy outcomes and business decisions. One doesn't have to look further for an example than the Australian federal government, which is anything but gender equal, and where, as a consequence, the 2020 budget was blind to the gendered impacts of the pandemic, focusing on a male-led economic recovery. Despite all this clear evidence, women in leadership so often find themselves the only woman in the room.

*

Most women, and I suspect some men, have been faced with the situation where they say something, it's not heard, and ten minutes later someone else says exactly the same thing and it's lauded as a good idea. Women and men are often talked over in meetings – but research has consistently found that men interrupt women far more than each other.

My friend and I met as colleagues and both sat on an Industry Association Committee meeting every month. We were the only women in this room of men. We both observed that at almost every meeting, one male committee member never said anything until after my friend and I spoke. Once we had spoken, he would paraphrase but essentially say exactly the same thing – to much praise and agreement from the rest of the committee.

When President Obama took office, his female staffers (outnumbered two to one) had trouble getting their voices heard in meetings, so they adopted what they dubbed an 'amplification' strategy: consistently repeating and acknowledging each other's key contributions in meetings.

'I'm speaking. Mr Vice President, I'm speaking' – those words were said at least four times during a ninety-minute presidential debate in 2020 by Kamala Harris, at the time the challenging US VP, to the then VP Mike Pence. Pence had persistently gone overtime during his time slots and interrupted Harris a total of ten times. It is no surprise that this caused a social media storm and resonated with women the world over. One very apt tweet was 'All women are Kamala today'.

In referring to a study about 'talking time' during meetings, the advice to men from a book co-authored by the twenty-seventh (and only woman) prime minister of Australia, Julia Gillard, is as follows: 'Ask yourself as you participate in discussions, am I talking or interrupting more than I should? Are the women not being heard? If the answer to either question is yes, level the playing field. If you are the one who determines how the meeting functions think about the decision-making model and how you equalise talking time.'

Our thirtieth prime minister, Scott Morrison, clearly didn't heed this advice. Quite the opposite – in fact, he cemented the reputation of his government's problem image when it comes to women in a demonstration of what has become known as a 'manterruption'. During a press conference held after the 2020 *Four Corners* episode 'Inside the Canberra Bubble', about power, sexism and inappropriate workplace conduct in government, a senior female minister was asked what the culture was like for women in politics. She was barely a few words into her answer when Morrison interrupted. He also dismissed what was inappropriate misconduct as 'human frailty'. It was almost parody in the circumstances – and attracted international headlines.

Ironically, aside from having more women in the room, it is the behaviour of leaders that is most important in amplifying voices in these situations.

For one of my first big deals in the corporate world, I was seated on one side of the oversized boardroom table together with three external expert consultants and advisors, my boss and the business unit director. All men. Seated opposite were five other men, including an interpreter. They were from Japan. I felt nervous but confident. *I've done all the work after all,* I thought to myself. *I'm probably the only person here who knows the contents of the 'data room' back to front.*

My boss and the consultants were dealing in the clunky way that a language barrier can impose on commercial negotiations. When the men opposite us reached a part in the process that they needed to discuss privately, they simply had the interpreter stop interpreting, and they turned and talked among themselves rather than leave the room. They obviously thought this was safe to do given the language barrier. What they didn't know, nor did I, was that the consultant seated next to me spoke fluent Japanese.

As they were talking, I noticed the men opposite were looking at me and laughing. The 'undercover linguist' consultant scribbled a note and handed it to me – he had translated what they were saying. I didn't really need the translation note; I'd read the nonverbal cues. 'They just said they want to know what the *pretty one* thinks on this issue …' I suspected from his look they had said something more.

That evening, our Japanese colleagues had invited everyone in the room to a dinner at one of Melbourne's finest restaurants, to which I'd never been, and I was looking forward to it. But my invitation was withdrawn late that afternoon. They had had a quiet word to my boss and said they didn't want a woman, the 'pretty one', at the dinner.

My boss openly rejected the withdrawal of my invitation, saying that I had done all the hard work and I should go. He had made it clear that if I was not invited then he wouldn't attend. Our teammates were annoyed with him, saying our visitors would take offence. In the end, the dinner simply went ahead without us.

I remember feeling grateful for being supported in this way. I know that many would regard it as a small gesture of principal. But this was the first time I realised what it meant to have a leader who supported your navigation around a roadblock, no matter how small. By standing up for me, my boss was likely taking some personal professional risk on himself, but if he hadn't have done that, it would have effectively conceded to the idea that, despite all my abilities and hard work, I was less entitled to respect and inclusion because I was a woman.

Once, as a young corporate lawyer, I presented a governance training session for a group of key external stakeholders. There were about thirty men in that room, and once again I was the only woman. At the conclusion of the presentation, I was accompanied to the door by the hosting junior executive, but as I exited the door remained ajar, and I was still within clear earshot as he turned back to the room and made a blokey, highly sexualised and sleazy comment about me and his consequent inability to concentrate – to which the response was uproarious loud collective male laughter. Granted, some of the men may have felt obliged to laugh because the joke was made by their boss.

One time, during a meeting of senior executives I was witness to a similar scenario with a different ending. This time there was me and one other woman in the room full of men. The other woman was making a presentation, accompanied by a senior male partner from one of the big four accounting firms. It was clear she had done all the work and was across the brief, and she answered all the questions assiduously. It was obvious that the male presenter was there merely because of his status as senior partner to 'impress the client'; he made minimal contributions to the presentation.

It was also obvious that she was an exceptionally attractive woman: slim, tall, very pretty and beautifully dressed. The senior partner was an overweight, balding white male, who wasn't doing a good job of faking that he was across the brief. As they left the room, this woman would have nearly experienced the same fate of collective male laughter as I had, as one of the executives around the boardroom table quipped 'Well – *he* was attractive …'

The chair of the meeting immediately stepped in, stern-faced, so that there was no chance for a spontaneous response and said, 'Let's go around the table starting with you,' he indicated the sexist joker, 'and discuss her excellent business presentation, which will help the company meet its strategy and vision.' The joker had nothing sensible to say.

If respect for women is demonstrated by all who participate in a meeting – or failing all, at least by the chair – then all voices are heard, and the meetings generally proceeded constructively towards strong outcomes. If respectful discussion is insisted upon, even when you're the only woman in the room, it makes a huge difference.

*

I don't ascribe to the theory that women tend to actively pit themselves against each other. It's yet another gender stereotype. Most women I know hugely value their friendships with other women in the workplace. I cannot even begin to imagine my life or career journey without the support of other women – and many of my enduring friendships with women started in the workplace.

That's not to say that female solidarity or the sisterhood prevails no matter what. It doesn't. Just as you can have bad male bosses and men who betray your trust, so it can be with women. Quite often, even when there's other women in the room, you can feel like you're the only one. Especially if they have aligned themselves with a patriarchal culture for the sake of their survival or progression. In the workplace, men and women can sometimes change when they get promoted.

Once, during my corporate career, the change in a woman who had been promoted was obvious to everyone on her team. People said she suddenly became 'not herself'. She took on characteristics that were more aligned with her male predecessor, who was aloof and brusque, as if she had to fit into his template of what leadership looked like.

Madeleine Albright made the famous statement that 'there is a special place in hell for women who don't help other women', which I really don't like. Why shouldn't it also apply to men? Moreover, it is saying that, once again, women should be the ones who must always blindly support other women. Albright's less famous statement is that there is a 'special place of honour' for women who support women. In fact, I think the better way to put it is that there's a special place of *honour* for women *and men* who support women.

It is not news that good leadership delivers success, and diverse leadership even more so. But it's not enough to say that, or to expect women to solve the problem themselves. Real structures you can touch and feel and that are supported by all is what will make the substantive changes we need to see.

In my time in politics, I experienced first-hand Niki Savva's observation that women of the Liberal Party were damned if they did and damned if they didn't: 'If they complained … they were ridiculed as being weak [or] condemned as wreckers and liars [as I was]. If they didn't, they knew an unsavoury culture … would continue.' I observed that the same women in the party who thought quotas were a 'Labor solution to a Liberal problem' or that they didn't want to be a 'quota girl', also thought the 'sisterhood' was a 'Labor thing' – or at least they feign this belief.

Although women in the Liberal Party generally won't openly talk about the 'women problem', they avidly use private female-MP-only meetings to air their grievances. Part of their fear of saying what they really think is a fear of being labelled a feminist – driven by the fact that such a label would compromise their support within the party or their preselection chances – or a fear for their careers more generally.

Only days after I had called out bullying and intimidation across the parties in my August 2018 media statement announcing I wasn't recontesting, one of the female Liberal MPs who had been openly seen by multiple MPs as distressed, crying and bullied into voting a certain way during the week of the leadership coup started publicly denying that there was any bullying, insisting rather that it was 'lobbying'. She told me and other MPs that she actually went ahead with this as she 'did a deal' for her preselection to be effectively endorsed on national television by a party powerbroker (one of the same members of the party who had told her how to vote during the coup, failing which her preselection would be 'severely compromised'). Essentially, she bolstered the narrative that I and other women who called out bullying – which she herself had encountered – were liars.

One vehicle intended to create a female support network in the party was a coalition women's WhatsApp group. It was originally intended to be used to organise the odd social event or share some parliamentary policy specific to women. But by default it contained exchanges that clearly referred to the 'women problem' and served as a kind of venting forum, where the women of the party all complained about the boys' behaviour, along the lines of: 'We, each of us, inspire young women to aim for leadership; how do we continue to do this in the face of puerile backstabbing from male party members whose aim is to count numbers and take our place?'

After the leadership coup had seen the toxic workplace culture magnified, the following message was sent to the group (with that faux-chirpy Stepford-wife tone of 'nothing to see here') by a female MP to whom many, including me, had confided in about workplace misconduct for years: 'Hello ladies, please come along to afternoon tea in my office after QT [Question Time] on Wednesday 12th – the first week back. Put it in your diaries and let me know whether you can come please. Look forward to seeing you soon!!'

I laughed out loud when I received this message. In attendance would have been the same female MPs who had 'done deals' with male leaders during the coup, and had complained about the workplace culture and behaviour but then gone 'internal' by the time parliament resumed in September.

The last thing I felt like was talking about the boys' club over a cup of tea and biscuits.

The same female MP who 'did the deal' to have her preselection endorsed was seemingly tasked to 'attack Banks' during the 2019 election, and praised for doing so – that she had 'taken on Banks' was 'to her great credit', a senior Liberal elder put it. She went so negative that I seriously contemplated taking legal action. Was her 'credit' the assistant ministry position she was rewarded with after the election? When speaking of her promotion, she said it was because of her skills and experience – that she was 'Not here because of [my] skirt' – and reinforced her support for the 'merit' argument. Even though, behind the scenes, speaking in our WhatsApp group about a female MP losing her preselection to a male, she said, '... my blood is boiling that a proven performer who happens also to be a woman was challenged in the first place, and ... those preselectors should never be allowed to utter the word "merit" again without being slapped.'

*

A lot of us have heard women say, 'I don't see any sexism.' And that may be a fact of their reality – but it's not the reality for most women in the workplace. Not everyone sees the biases and discrimination that hold them or their colleagues back in their career trajectories, at every stage. Sometimes it's imperceptible. You don't see it until you reflect back on it, or you subconsciously don't want to see it. You might only experience it at certain stages of your career – for example, when you take parental leave.

In the corporate world, much is often invested in women's leadership development, formal mentoring programs and the like.

Business texts, consultants, executive leadership conferences and forums abound with advice about the importance of role models, sponsors, referees, support people, counsellors and networking forums. I have personally benefitted from all these things and enjoyed returning the favour. But while all of it can be helpful, affirming and even cathartic, they do not go far enough on their own.

One of the downsides with a lot of these vehicles is that the only people in the room are women. As Catherine Fox points out in *Stop Fixing Women*, it is 'mainly women who are involved in diversity projects and mentoring networks while men at the top are busy making the decisions that have the greatest impact.' Quite often, speakers at these events will specifically congratulate and praise the men for attending at all.

Fox also describes other types of formal programs: 'Mentoring has largely failed to deliver change. Instead, sponsorship is viewed as being much more likely to progress gender balance … Diversity councils can be useful … [but] some are little more than window dressing.'

Fox's opinions on mentoring were supported by a *Harvard Business Review* article, which suggested that instead of 'mentors', you should look for 'champions': people who actually make things happen for you.

I always remember an interaction I had with a young woman who requested that I be her 'new mentor' in a formal mentoring program. In our first coffee meeting, she explained how grateful she was but how awkward she'd felt as she'd had to ask her boss to change her mentor from one of the male senior executives in the company to me.

Knowing this male senior executive personally, and knowing he was a professional, personable, great leader, I was curious and asked, 'Why did you ask for the change?'

She replied, 'I am struggling with a new family and demands of my work. I was seeking his mentorship about balance. He slowly but surely started coaching and mentoring me to become like his wife, who has children the same age and has given up her career, and I couldn't think of anything worse.'

I'm sure that my 'championing' this woman's skills to her superiors had a far greater impact on her career than our 'mentoring' coffee chats.

McKinsey's annual 'Women in the Workplace' report included these lines in 2019: 'Many companies need to do more to put their commitment into practice and treat gender diversity like the business priority it is. This starts with taking concrete actions like setting diversity targets and sharing diversity metrics – not just at senior levels, but with all employees.'

There is plenty of evidence of businesses increasing their success by creating targets for numbers of senior women. Personally, on my leadership journey, I have seen the implementation of incentivised targets change the gender balance at senior levels. Making an equal number of women in leadership directly tied to key performance indicators works. Arguments in support of the meritocracy are already proven to be hopelessly flawed, as promotion based on merit is impeded by bias and discrimination – whether overt or unconscious. The proof is in the pudding. If the merit argument were true in a population that is roughly fifty/fifty men and women, it would follow that there are more meritorious men in our society than there are women. I don't doubt that some people in business actually believe this to be true, but as long as we let those biases continue to shape our workplaces unchecked, without the structural measures to counter them, we won't be able to disprove it. So far, the focus on gender balance in the corporate sector has been largely at the senior director levels, but the more strategic organisations are starting at the beginning, at graduate and entry level.

Nowhere are the discrepancies of women in leadership more obvious – or more important – than in politics. In the history of Australian federal politics, 1205 people have been elected to the House of Representatives. Of those 1205, only 133 are women, of which I'm very proud to have been one. But 133 is clearly not enough. In the World Economic Forum's Global Gender Gap Report, where nations are ranked in terms of gender equality on a political and social and economic level, Australia has dropped to fifty. New Zealand is ranked fourth. Australia lagging so far behind is woeful, disturbing and needs urgent attention.

Targets work in business, and only quotas will do in politics. Mandatory quotas will be a circuit-breaker towards equal representation across the political divide. Granted, this is more than a numbers game. While not the panacea, having equal numbers of men and women in our federal parliament will change the culture and the dialogue, and it will lead to better policy outcomes and better decisions being made by people with different lived experiences.

Having introduced quotas in 1994, nearly a quarter of a century ago, the Labor Party has proven that a quota system works to get numbers up, even if it's a long process. At the same time that Labor now have close to parity with men and women, the Liberals languish at 23 per cent.

But while the Liberal Party are comfortable with quotas with regard to geography and a balance between National and Liberal ministers, they have consistently maintained their obstinate and vocal objection to quotas only when it comes to gender. The Liberal Party aligned Menzies Research Centre 2020 report rejected quotas as 'unpalatable' and 'undemocratic'.

Throughout my tenure with the Liberal Party, my preference for quotas was always met with a solid rejection or (particularly from some of the women who had been there longer than me) a hushed warning not to mention the Q-word.

A backbencher is given allocated 'speech opportunities', and in the sitting weeks after the 2018 coup that saw Morrison take over the leadership from Turnbull, it seemed I was being given these opportunities at the end of the day or at times when no one would be paying attention. One of my speech opportunities was scheduled for the night of the Midwinter Ball, when the press gallery and MPs converge in the Great Hall together; because of everything that had transpired after the coup, I had decided not to attend. My speech that night was about quotas – and I felt like I was the only woman in the chamber.

Some female MPs heard about the speech and gave me a hug on their way to the Great Hall, and journalists were texting me from the ball.

The next day it was all over the press, which of course displeased the powers that be. I was soon fielding calls from Murdoch journalists who said they had been newly briefed by 'senior Liberal sources' that I was 'a bully' and a 'nasty woman' during the 2016 campaign.

In March 2021, after weeks of unrelenting scandal and pressure regarding sexism and misogyny in the Australian parliament, Scott Morrison said he was 'open to the conversation' about quotas. I'm all for people admitting they've changed their mind, but Morrison didn't do this. I know I'm not the only person who saw this as a meaningless tactic to drown out media commentary about the real issues facing his leadership and the political storm hitting his government. And then, suddenly, female MPs have emerged, speaking as if he has given permission that they could at least also be 'open to' quotas.

The whole debate about quotas in the Liberal Party reminds me of a grim but enduring moment when I was sitting next to former Foreign Minister Julie Bishop in the party room in Parliament House, minutes after she'd lost her tilt for leadership during the 2018 coup.

Morrison rose to his feet, his buoyancy at his new-found status making him oblivious to the bloodshed that had just been caused. He addressed the party room with a weird combination of evangelical fervour and 'footy coach trying to rev up the boys after a bad game'.

He pointed excitedly to the framed photographs of all the previous male leaders and prime ministers of the party. And then in a final flourish he added, with an attempted 'worldly' tone, '… and one day there will be a woman there.'

Julie Bishop, renowned for her impeccable comeback lines, metaphorically pushed Morrison off his pulpit with her quiet quip: 'In which century?'

Not long after the coup, I attended the unveiling of the portrait of our first female prime minister, Julia Gillard, in the mural room at Parliament House. It should go without saying that the unveiling of a portrait in Parliament House is viewed as an important moment and traditionally proceeds with a respectful bi-partisan celebration. I was ashamed but not surprised that the newly installed prime minister and most of his ministers didn't attend. I was honoured to go. Aside from the natural expectation that I should attend the celebration, as any member of parliament should, this was our first female prime minister, and I had never met her.

Upon being unveiled, the portrait drew audible gasps from the audience; it is a beautiful work of art by Vincent Fantauzzo. I was struck (as I'm sure others were) by its stark difference to every other prime minister's portrait – not least because it was the only one of a woman.

Gillard said in her speech that she looked forward to a time when there were more female PMs in that mural room, and that she had been encouraged to believe in the nearness of that time by the recent 'lively debate' in politics. Lively debate that I'd certainly been a part of, in speaking out against the anti-woman culture in Parliament House and calling for quotas – sparking a groundswell of vitriol.

I stood in the queue for my chance to meet our only female prime minister, and when it came my turn, the cameras started clicking furiously. I had no doubt the microphones were on, so I leaned in towards her, and whispered my thanks for 'everything she had done for women'.

She warmly whispered back, while we were still shaking hands, 'You know how to get my number – if you want a confidential chat.'

No doubt the cynics would have something to say about that gesture, but for me it was embracing and generous. Despite everything that was happening at the time, and everything that happened to her during her term, she made a gesture of warmth and empathy, which touched me deeply. Despite the obvious difference in our politics and political status, I felt at that moment we had a shared connection, as two women who know what it's like to experience misogyny in the public arena.

Feeling like you are the only woman or indeed *being* the only woman in the room sadly creates silence, rather than 'lively debate'. But lively debate is well overdue if we want to see meaningful structural change from all leaders in all sectors. We require actions that ensure that all voices, both male and female, are equally heard.

When it comes to politics, these actions are urgent imperatives, because we need the centre of power in our country to be made up of representatives of the lived experiences of men and women equally.

And we need more portraits of female prime ministers hanging in our federal parliament.

Chapter 7

Never too old

'How old *are* you?' No, we're not back at that political preselection interview. This time I was working in a corporate role, bantering with a senior HR executive as we sat opposite each other in the new-fangled open-plan system that felt more 'call centre' than executive suite, so everyone could overhear the conversation. He'd only recently been promoted, and while his promotion didn't give him a corner office, his new-found status gave him unfettered access to all employee records, including mine.

He knew he couldn't ask that question, and seemingly put it to me as a joke. So, I 'joked' back. 'That's an illegal question. The HR guy shouldn't ask the chief general counsel illegal questions.'

'Come on … how old are you?' he persisted, like he had a right to know and he couldn't be bothered accessing the records.

'I'm the same age as Demi Moore,' I said, giving him a visual rather than a metric, while still looking more interested in the emails on my screen. I wasn't going to make life easy for him. I could have said I was like him and middle-aged – I was roughly ten years older, but I recalled that a British survey does put middle age between thirty-seven and fifty-eight.

Thanks to my public profile since entering politics, my 'age' is available for all to see. No more putting people to the inconvenience of searching 'Demi Moore age' on the internet. Up until that point, I always resented giving my age, not because I'd feel old, but because I knew that questions about a woman's age are almost always seeking to enable some kind of prejudiced judgement. Age is probably one of the most critical data points in a woman's working life that causes bias and discrimination – we know it's the case for young women, but it's also the case as women grow older.

The truth is, I don't know what it's like to 'feel old'. If to feel old is to feel chronically tired, then I certainly *felt* older in my mid-thirties, when I was raising two children and working, than I do now, some twenty-plus years later.

I'm sure some people would assume that, having faced the possibility of the 'alternative to ageing' in my late twenties, I would have a healthy perspective on ageing. But I think that saying ageing is better than the alternative is a bleak and depressing way to approach things.

Ageing is part of life. It's going through life. And just as there are highlights and lowlights in life, so there are in ageing.

I was once out for a rushed lunch with a good friend. She's much younger than me, but her work and family life are almost identical to mine at the same age.

She was still being asked all the questions: *Why aren't you home with the children? Why are you working full-time? How much mat leave are you taking? Are you having more children? Why? Why not?*

And then she kept asking herself (albeit guiltily, because the perception was that she had it all), *Is this … it?*

She was grappling with her next steps. In the context of our broad-ranging discussion of our doubts, uncertainties, ambivalences and choices, she asked me a question: 'What would you advise your thirty-five-year-old self?'

She asked the question with a look of hope in her eyes, as if willing me to give her the answer to her own troubles in a couple of profound sentences – like in one of those magazine profiles. At first, I was stumped. But then I said, 'Just do what you want to do. Just keep pushing through. Weigh up the consequences – for you – of each decision, and then do what your heart tells you.'

In retrospect I wish I had answered by drawing inspiration from Dame Helen Mirren. When the seventy-something Oscar-winning icon was asked in an interview in 2017 what she would say to her younger self, she replied, 'Say "fuck off" more and stop being so bloody polite'.

It's sort of the same advice as I gave my younger friend – Helen Mirren just conveyed it a little more succinctly. The only bit I'd add is you don't always have to say it, you can just think it – and then do what you want to do. It does make you feel better.

I sacked my favourite hairdresser when I was thirty-eight. Not in an all-guns-blazing kind of way, I just never went back – and it wasn't because he'd made a mess of my haircut. I had been going to him since my early thirties, through both pregnancies, and I even took my toddlers to him for their first haircuts.

But as I sat down for my usual 'just a trim', he stood back and said, 'Can I suggest something?'

'Sure', I said, interested in a new style idea.

'I think it's time for you to cut your hair short.'

I was open to the idea of a creative suggestion for a new look and style based on his expertise. But before we got into discussing it any further, he muttered the 'sackable' words: 'It will look more age appropriate.'

Age appropriate. A phrase I've never understood. I probably attribute this to my mother's attitude to ageing. To this day I still love clothes shopping with my mother. When, in her late seventies, she bought a classy pair of leopard-print trousers, a few of her friends baulked. I was proud.

Rather than quietly not make another appointment with my hairdresser ever again, I wish I'd adopted the Helen Mirren approach.

In my late forties I was chairing a business meeting during the horrendous time of perimenopause. The headache-to-migraine journey was happening all too frequently. I've always suffered from migraines and still do, but during perimenopause and menopause, the intensity and frequency coupled with every other symptom you could think of was something else.

This time, the migraine was compounded by the fact that I felt like I was trapped in an overheated sauna. A hot flush is an insufficient term for what can actually happen. Americans diminish the description even more, by calling it a 'hot flash', like it's there and then not there like the quick pin-prick of an injection. They can happen with the intensity of a roaring fire sweeping through your body. They can sneak up on you, wake you up in the night and come in waves of such frequency that you barely have time to recover.

On this occasion, the burning sensation stopped as I surreptitiously wiped my forehead, but the migraine pain wasn't lifting, it was getting worse, and consequently my sense of anxiety was deepening. *I'm going to have to leave work. Again*, I thought.

I got through the meeting. Only right at the end, as we left the meeting room did one of my more observant direct reports picked up on something being wrong. Bless him, yes *him*, he got me a glass of water and asked, 'Are you okay?'

'I'm getting a migraine ... need to get home. Can you hold the fort for me?' I was glad I could get the words out without sounding like I was having a stroke.

I got in the car (which in retrospect was not a great idea) and focused on getting home before it took hold. I felt paresthesia and tingling in my left arm just as I pulled up in the driveway. I got inside, drew the curtains for the relief of darkness, took some medication and fell into bed. I flicked a text to a colleague in London to advise him that we'd have to postpone our evening conference call to the next day because I was sick.

Throughout their decades, women often experience absences from the workplace in a way that men don't. This could be due to their menstrual cycle, having children, caring responsibilities, perimenopause, menopause, going part-time or after having negotiated remote working. I remember being struck the first time I noticed a man experiencing the anxiety that absence from the workplace can cause. In line with his law firm's policy, this man was forced to take a three-month sabbatical, and he became visibly anxious and vocally very concerned that the substitute partner or someone else would 'take his clients'. That feeling – that an absence will mean your job is threatened or that someone is waiting in the wings to make a move on it – is often inevitably felt by women when their absence is necessary, no matter how temporary.

Soon after the day of the migraine, I saw the same London-based colleague face to face at an international conference in Asia: a conference that often determined visibility for career trajectories, promotions and opportunities. It was all going swimmingly, and then, on day two of the conference, that familiar migraine plus roaring fire feeling swept over me in the afternoon. I escaped to the sanctuary of my hotel room at a time of day when things were winding down anyway and no-one would really notice. Or so I thought.

After I'd slept it off for a couple of hours, I checked my phone and found a few messages of 'concern' from my London colleague. I called him back.

He empathised. 'Nothing worse than being sick when you're away from home. Once I had the flu …' Yadda yadda yadda. On he droned, and I had to keep listening to him while being grateful that this was just a phone call. At least I didn't have to make my face feign interest in the melodrama of his historical case of 'man flu' while in the midst of my own post-migraine haze.

Then he obviously remembered my cancelled conference call and said, 'Look, don't worry. If I'm asked why you get sick all the time, I'll just say you're always "absent from class" because you're at an age where you have a "very weak disposition".' He chuckled, ostensibly joking.

This colleague was senior to me, younger than me, but by virtue of a unique matrix leadership structure, we had the same boss. One night after a few too many drinks, our mutual boss had told me that, from the time I first came on board, the London guy had seen me as a threat competing for his London post, based on my extensive experience compared to his, and especially given my family connections to England and the fact that I travelled there regularly. Certainly, his general attitude towards me had been consistent with this.

Menopause and perimenopause can make work a struggle for women, but it's still a taboo issue – perhaps even more so than other women's biological health issues, such as menstrual health. It coincides with a time in women's careers when they're at the precipice of becoming the CEO or making that final leap to the top. It can cause significant need to be absent from work, and it is therefore one of the reasons that men in power can overlook women for that 'ultimate promotion' and a reason competing men use to somehow win the race.

Even though 'there's always one' – or ten – people within your workplace that can make life difficult (as I found with my London colleague), I was fortunate that I always worked for organisations that put their employees' health and safety at a premium, and supported women and men alike. But not all women are so lucky. A 2020 report surveying 2000 British doctors found that most received no employer support when it came to managing menopause symptoms. We have only in recent times started to recognise that menstrual leave is a good thing. Menopause leave could be added to that. I believe a better solution would be to make our workplace leave policies in employment more flexible in general.

Symptoms of menopause can vary in frequency, intensity and type for women. Some women barely notice they've gone through menopause. Sometimes the symptoms can be severe: on top of hot flushes, headaches and migraines, they can include anxiety, depression, brain fog and weakened short-term memory. This necessarily will often result in absences from work or a decline in performance at work, and likely also exacerbates the invisibility of women in the workplace at a time when they should be reaching these positions of power.

Invisibility is a common depiction of middle-aged women. And not just because of the way men's heads might no longer turn. After consulting a panel of fifty women for her book *The Shift*, Sam Baker concluded that 'When people talk about not being whistled at by builders anymore – that's not the point, the point is suddenly men with the exact same CV are being made CEOs and you're just … disappearing.' Baker notes that where older men are considered to have 'valuable professional experience', some older women were told they were now 'too expensive to hire': 'Their children were no longer taking up all their time and they were all like: "Great, what next?" And the world's response is: "Oh, is that grey hair? No thanks."'

One of the darkest outcomes of the cultural invisibility of older women is that, after years of government policy inaction on systemic gender discrimination in the workplace, women over the age of fifty-five are now Australia's fastest-growing homeless population group and those facing a life of poverty. This has been magnified during the pandemic. Meanwhile, men over fifty-five are often in the prime of their careers.

*

When I became an MP, people were split between being curious, admiring and horrified that I made such a career change. Many said things along the lines of 'That's such a big call,' and, 'Why leave a perfectly good, high-paying career?' Several actually outright asked me 'Why do this now, at your age?'

A key factor in my decision was actually related to my age. Because of my years of work, I was at a stage in my life where my financial security was sorted and I could take this risk. I was genuinely curious to see what it was like on the inside of politics. I'd always integrated my advocacy on issues that were important to me into my business life, and now the Liberal Party were publicly calling for more women. Their values of individual enterprise resonated with me, I saw leaders in the party (all of whom have now left) whose socially progressive and economically conservative views aligned with mine, and I thought this might present an opportunity to continue my advocacy on a broader platform.

So, in my early fifties and for the first time in my life, I joined a political party.

At the time of joining in 2015, I had no idea that I would be making my maiden speech in parliament the following year.

In line with a kind of unspoken 'gender discriminatory tradition' held by both the major parties, when I joined the Liberal Party I was approached to run for preselection in a marginal seat, regarded as unwinnable as it had been held by the opposition for close to twenty years. I was told with an air of certainty, 'You won't even win preselection, because you're new ... but it's only a six-minute speech, and it's a good way to network and get to know people in the party.' One branch official, noting the sheer impossibility of the potential to win the seat said, 'If you win the seat, they'll make you prime minister.' Haha.

It all sounded sensible, and easy. But it was actually an intense period of networking, night-time and weekend phone calls, and constantly meeting people. I worked my 'two jobs' concurrently for a period when I was a candidate, until the intensive eighteen-hour days of doing my day job of company director/general counsel and then campaigning in the remaining waking hours became too much. I made an incredibly difficult choice to resign from my day job a few months before the election. It meant no certainty of the next step, but I figured, *Win or lose, I'll want a break, and it's not fair to my employer to ask for extended leave.*

Effectively, from the time I was preselected, for a period of nine months, I was working day and night, voluntarily, for the Liberal Party. This made the relentless and constant undermining I received from within the party in this time even more difficult to tolerate. It was often brutal, sometimes absurdly trivial, but always personal and highly disrespectful – I don't know how many times I was told I was not up to the job. One member told me that at my age, I would have seen so many elections, and she couldn't believe I'd never handed out a single brochure for other politicians.

Alarmingly, all this undermining only increased after I was preselected. At a public forum meeting, an audience of the party faithful were told aggressively that I was 'so inexperienced because she is so new to the party,' like it was a massive performance issue on my part. To be called 'inexperienced' with my age and experience was borderline ridiculous, but the speaker demonstrated what he really meant when he once told me, 'You're managing this like you're a fucking CEO.' Clearly, he felt my corporate leadership skills were a bad thing. I took it as a compliment. Personally, I will always believe that my corporate leadership and managerial experience – years of fine-tuning how to lead a team and meet goals – was not only my point of difference from the career candidates and politicians, it was one of the main reasons we won the unwinnable seat.

When I asked when I would be speaking on the program for a Liberal fundraising event, I was told, 'Don't you worry, darlin'. We'll give you the raffle.'

I was given advice on campaigning: 'You should be campaigning for better toilet blocks in the local shopping centre – stop rabbiting on about the economy. Leave that to the big boys.'

One local branch official told me that I would be a 'fucking hopeless MP' if I couldn't *lie*, and yelled at me that I was a 'useless candidate' and a 'pighead' in my own home – so loudly that my son, studying in his bedroom, came running downstairs to check if everything was okay.

I was told by more than one federal MP that the Victorian Division HQ had advised the federal campaign 'not to bother' with me as a candidate because 'she was useless' and 'just a crazy corporate woman'.

Just prior to the election, I sent an email to two of the men employed by the Victorian Division HQ to work on my campaign, requesting for them to amend a media release that was grammatically incorrect and could have been misinterpreted. One of them hit 'reply all', but his message was obviously just intended for his 'partner in crime': 'I suppose you'll roll over and give your girlfriend what she wants.'

This was brought to the attention of the state director, who said he had told the official it was 'unacceptable' and that 'he was mortified ... He will ring to apologise.' Needless to say, I didn't answer his call. It was the usual story. They're only 'mortified' because they've been found out.

Two days after Christmas in 2015, I received a phone call from a twenty-something, perennially unemployed male young Liberal. I had heard that he had been telling anyone in the party who would listen that in his opinion after 'observing me' he would be the better candidate, even though months earlier he hadn't bothered to run for preselection. I answered the call knowing he wasn't genuinely interested in how my Christmas had been. He explained his heartfelt desire for me to stand down and gift my candidacy to him because he was young and energetic, and had the party values in his heart and soul.

As his final flourish, he said earnestly, 'You can't campaign and win this while having such a big job and career. Someone your age wouldn't have the energy anyway.'

Astoundingly, this same young Liberal later applied for a job in my office after I was elected. I did the polite thing and pretended to give consideration to his application, returned his call and let him down gently. Now I wish I'd just sent him a text a la Helen Mirren's advice: 'Fuck off.'

I tolerated all these jabs and bullying by maintaining my focus on the end-goal. I'd earned my ticket on this road, and I developed a steely determination to see the opportunity through.

The attacks were a consistent backdrop throughout the campaign. Even on election day. A party branch official who had a role to man a polling booth arrived at my campaign office and said to another volunteer, 'I suppose I should take an A-frame, but no one's going to vote for that old bitch anyway.' We found out he left the polling booth by midday, so my family and friends frantically organised to fill his role. My 'they won't break me' brand of determination was well-honed by then, but I was incredulous that even on this day these people, in my own party, were willing, assuming and/or conniving for my failure. That night, together with my family, friends, loyal supporters and team, we proved them wrong.

We won the unwinnable seat.

During our dual corporate career period, my husband and I got invited to numerous events 'with partners' all the time. We made a deliberate decision to rarely go to each other's functions. We regarded these as part of our jobs, and we both strongly believed that we weren't automatic extensions of each other's job descriptions. We much preferred to let each other talk shop in our own shop and socialise with our own work colleagues, clients or customers. It got to the point where my colleagues joked about my 'fictional husband' because he was so rarely dragged along to my employer's functions, and vice versa.

But for the first Midwinter Ball at Parliament House, we made an exception to our secret policy and I bought two tickets for us. Because I was new to the game, we got seated at a table largely with people we didn't know, including other MPs who, like me, had just been elected for the first time. Their partners had also accompanied them.

I'd barely sat down and done the artificial around-the-table introductions, when a newly minted male MP from the opposition sitting across from me said, 'Julia, I've been meaning to say to you – you must use a really strong hair dye?'

Undoubtedly this was a dig at my being a woman of a certain age. For the record, my natural hair colour is 'regular dark brown', but I use a colour to cover the grey roots. Unashamedly. I prefer the look of regular dark brown hair, without the grey – just like I prefer to wear make-up when I'm out.

I thought afterwards that what I could have said in reply to that balding middle-aged MP was, 'At least I've got hair.' Or maybe I should have just used the Helen Mirren approach again.

Instead, I turned to the woman next to me, who hadn't heard that little exchange. *She'll be more polite*, I thought, but I should have seen her first icebreaker question coming at me. 'Which electorate is your husband the MP for?'

Am I in a 1950s movie, rather than in the Great Hall of Parliament House in 2016? Get me out of here! I thought. But I replied, surprising myself with my nonchalance, 'I'm the MP here. He's my handbag, like you are to your husband.'

That probably caused an 'ouch' moment for her. But again, the Helen Mirren approach would have made me happiest.

What I had to put up with as a woman in politics with respect to my age is nothing short of staggering, especially since, during my term, Australia was one of the first countries in the world to have an organisation dedicated to addressing ageism, Every Age Counts.

Soon after the election, a number of MPs set up the 'Class of 2016': a group where new MPs from that year could socialise together. At first, I thought the name was both infantile and elitist – a bit 'private boys' school yearbook' – but the concept was a good idea: we would take turns to host an evening, either in our office or at a restaurant. It added to the camaraderie and was all built on us getting to know each other.

One night after a Class of 2016 dinner in one MP's office, two male MPs and I were sitting together just having a discussion about policies and life in general. Then, out of the blue, one MP said to the other, 'You would make such a great attorney-general. I can see you being attorney-general in a few years.' This was to a guy who had barely practised law in his short career.

But the mutual admiration society continued. 'No,' said the other with a tone of false modesty, 'I think you would, you articulate yourself so well in the media.'

'Aww thanks,' said the first MP, 'but I'm not a lawyer.' *Too bad that's a pretty important prerequisite to being the country's attorney-general,* I thought. He did have an ego so large it was almost visible.

Like all women I know, I'd been spoken over at board meetings, suggested great ideas and had them ignored and then stolen by someone else, and been mistaken for the assistant. I wasn't going to sit here in silence. 'Yeah, I mean my twenty-plus years of legal practice in the highest position of the legal profession in large corporates wouldn't really cut it.'

In their mind, I was invisible.

As I took that last sip of red wine and bid goodbye to my fellow aspiring attorneys-general, leaving them to clean up and do the dishes, my thought bubble was very Helen Mirren.

One of those same first-term MPs had their nose put out of joint when Turnbull appointed me as chair of the Social Policy and Legal Affairs Committee. I was also a member of the House Economics Committee, of which another female MP was appointed chair. These appointments are prestigious, only made by the prime minister, and often seen as a precursor to ministerial appointments. A female MP who held an MBA was once denied a spot on the House Economics Committee under the leadership of the previous prime minister, Tony Abbott; she was told she wasn't one of the '"big boys" who had PhDs and masters in economics'.

Apparently, several male MPs who missed out on getting on these committees took great umbrage at my appointments, and did not have the same regard for my corporate business experience as Turnbull did. Was it professional jealousy? Was it simply because I took their spot? Was it because I was a first-term, 'inexperienced' MP who held a marginal seat? Was it because I was a woman of a certain age? It was hard to say, as all these reasons were mentioned to me at one time or another.

The aspiring attorney-general MP with no law degree called me out of the blue when he'd 'heard whispers' about the appointments of myself and the other female MP on the House Economics Committee. 'You should both be focused on your marginal seats,' he bellowed down the phone, like the spoilt boy who missed out on the school prize.

'Us women learn to multitask in our old age. I think we can cope,' I said, in a tone that was a hybrid between being maternal and patronising – with just a hint of Helen Mirren.

What comes with age is certain resilience from the sense that you've 'seen it all'. But I never felt that during my time in politics. I was always on high alert for what might happen next, particularly because of the power of the some of the senior state-based leaders. By early 2018, rumours abounded that they were mobilising to challenge me (and other moderates) at the next preselection – despite my having won the marginal seat that secured majority government.

Preselection relies on local party member votes, and suddenly I was seeing increasing numbers of new members 'signing up' in my electorate. When I called them, many just hung up or didn't even know who I was; a few confessed that they 'weren't really sure' why they joined except that they 'did it for' the woman who was to be my successor.

This candidate was endorsed and supported by another Victorian MP. When I rang to challenge this MP about this situation, he aggressively said, 'Let me just interrupt you there. This is a very damaging phone call for you.'

I was incredulous: *They really do kill their own*. I turned the conversation around to seemingly end things politely, but of course I should have just used the Helen Mirren advice.

*

In a scene from the cult-hit television show *Fleabag*, there is an interaction between a thirty-three-year-old woman, played by Phoebe Waller-Bridge, and a fifty-eight-year-old woman she's just met, played by Kristin Scott Thomas. Scott Thomas's character delivers an incredible monologue. 'Women are born with pain … We carry it within ourselves throughout our lives. Men don't … We have pain on a cycle for years and years and years and then just when you feel you are making peace with it all, what happens? The menopause comes, the fucking menopause comes … It is horrendous … and then it's magnificent.'

The speech has tens of thousands of views on YouTube. Women everywhere responded to this remarkable monologue, which is one of the few instances where older women are depicted in popular culture as having something to want and aspire to – in particular, the strength and courage you can get with age.

Some have mused that women become more feminist with

age, and therefore more activist. But what does being 'more feminist' mean? You feel more strongly than you did when you were younger about equal rights? Or is it that you simply have more space freed up in your life to say what you think?

I've discussed the downsides of menopause in the workplace – but personally, for me, and I know for hundreds of other women, there's an upside. My theory for why women might seem more feminist as they age is explained by what I'm here and now going to name PMS 2.0: Post-Menopausal Superpower.

Organisations in any sector, and specifically men in power, should never underestimate a woman with PMS 2.0. By the time women get PMS 2.0, many have their own personal financial security sorted and a strong sense of their own power, their own self-worth. These women have been there, seen it, done it. And they damn well storm through any barriers. I think that's why that *Fleabag* monologue has such a cult following. Post-menopause, 'you're just a person – in business … It is horrendous, but then it's magnificent.' Try to stop these women at your peril. Criticise them, abuse them and mock them, and they will know that the problem is you and not them.

When I became an independent MP, the support I had from the other female independents, all aged between forty and seventy, was extraordinary. Our force was seen as a threat. Tactics were used by our opponents and enemies during the campaign to discredit us and diminish our power. I'm guessing that, given our 'mature age', they thought their focus should be on professional attacks rather than sexual smear campaigns.

As a result of the balance of power, the 'medevac' legislation came through which enabled passing the bill that allowed people in offshore detention requiring urgent medical attention to be transferred to Australia for this purpose. When the vote came down, all the MPs on the crossbench, without whom it wouldn't have passed, spontaneously and joyously responded. The two men on the crossbench stood up and shook hands, smiling broadly. The two other female crossbench MPs and I did the same – and then had a group hug. The front page of the Murdoch press the next day was a photo in which the two men had been removed so that it was an image of the three women hugging and smiling. The headline was the 'Grin Reapers'.

Then, during the 2019 campaign, an article published once again under the Murdoch banner (written by a disgruntled ex-staffer of former PM Tony Abbott) described the female independents under a blaring headline 'Labor mutton dressed as Liberal lamb'.

Again and again our critics, in parliament and in the media, men and women alike, relied on the ageist approach in their attacks. But I believe we not only had the balance of power in the House of Representatives, but we also had a unique power that comes with being older women with lived experience.

After my unsuccessful bid at the 2019 federal election, I issued a media statement that included the words 'You don't own me. You never did. And I don't owe a debt to you. It's a free country for people to run for office and to advocate for what they believe in.'

Those words were written in response to the general public criticism I'd received from Liberals, including current and former members of parliament, and the boys' club oracle John Howard, who said that I owed 'a lot' to the Liberal Party.

Those words were also inspired by the 1960s song 'You Don't Own Me' by Lesley Gore, who died in 2015 – the year I joined the Liberal Party. Along with the iconic 'I Am Woman' by Helen Reddy, Lesley Gore's was a song that I played over and over through my airpods as I was exercising to relieve the stress from the toxic culture I was immersed in.

Although my return to non-political life was a comfort to me, I did tire of a new question, often asked rhetorically, loaded with judgement and expectation. 'What next? Are you going to retire now?'

I was sharing my annoyance at this type of questioning with a dear friend of the same age, similarly experienced, who'd left an employer where she spent most of her career and was in the throes of doing other amazing things. She advised me, 'Just say you're taking a gap year. It makes you feel young, and it stops people in their tracks' – likely because a gap year is usually something people take *before* they get started in the real life of work. My friend continued, 'They know you can do all sorts of different things, things you love, in a gap year. And you're never too old to take a gap year ...'

Brilliant advice.

During my gap year and into the present, I've continued my work though my own business consultancy, speaking engagements, advocacy and taking up external appointments. I've continued my love for travel (pre-pandemic and in the context of COVID-19 restrictions) and embraced my love for cooking with a vengeance (especially during the pandemic – yes, I baked bread).

Once, at a retirement farewell dinner for a dear work colleague, I asked his wife how she felt about her husband retiring. 'Well Julia, it's half the money and twice the man.' But many people, when they retire, semi-retire or leave their professional careers, really feel the changes, such as less travelling and less social interaction, and have to adjust to a new daily life. Many say 'the phone stops ringing'. One retired politician coined the term 'relevance deprivation syndrome'.

There are definitely less phone rings and message pings in my life these days. But in the course of my career, I've left multiple jobs or workplaces, and I've never felt deprived of relevance – including when I left politics.

Rather, I've always just got on with the next thing.

Another question I still get is, 'Will you run as an independent again?' My answer: never say never. In the words of George Bernard Shaw, 'We don't stop playing because we grow old. We grow old because we stop playing.'

Chapter 8

To speak or not to speak

'Should I say something?' This question has entered the minds of most women, because most women have experienced or witnessed sexism, bullying, harassment and abuse.

Another question, asked less often: 'Why is it the woman's burden to tell uncomfortable stories when they have done nothing wrong?'

This question is posed in Jodi Kantor and Megan Twohey's book *She Said* about the Harvey Weinstein sexual harassment story that helped ignite the #MeToo movement. That burden of telling the stories and speaking up is underpinned by a very real fear: that you won't be believed. Fear that the perpetrators and their supporters will begin a narrative or scenario that discredits you or your reputation. Fear that you'll lose your job or risk your career path. Fear that the process is often more traumatic and distressing than the complaint itself. As Kantor and Twohey explained, they intended even the title of their book, *She Said*, to be 'a complicated one: We write about those who did speak out, along with others who chose not to, and the nuances of how when and why.'

Several years ago, I was in the beautiful Victorian countryside on a three-day trip. Not for pleasure, but for business – a strategic planning meeting for a large group of senior executives. At the time, I'd barely noticed that I was in the minority as a woman. Or perhaps I had become used to the scenario.

After a gruelling day of PowerPoint slides, discussions and morning and afternoon tea breaks in which the work talk continued apace, I was looking forward to the more relaxed dinner and drinks with my fellow team members. It was a balmy evening and, being a midweek event, we had the small conference venue to ourselves, including, once the hospitality staff left after the dinner, an open, self-managed bar. As the evening progressed, people slowly but surely started retiring. I became conscious of some important emails waiting for me that I knew I wouldn't have a chance to look at the next day because of the packed agenda. I also knew they would be best done if I didn't have that extra glass of wine. I bid goodnight to the remaining people, went to my room, made a cup of herbal tea, got into my PJs and settled at the desk. As I tapped away on my laptop, I was barely conscious of the sound of my happy colleagues' drinking and laughter slowly receding to a few voices, and then silence.

Suddenly, the silence was brutally broken by a frantic banging on my door, so forceful that the door flung open. I'm normally obsessive about locking doors at night, but I mustn't have locked it properly. I'd felt safe out there in the country with my trusted work colleagues.

Now I felt the opposite of safe. Standing in the doorway was one of my colleagues, an unusually large and very tall man who perpetually looked angry with the world. He matched that with a booming voice and an overly combative nature. This was on a good day … and when he was sober. Now he was drunk, and all his characteristics were amplified.

Startled, I quite literally jumped out of my seat, almost flew to grab the now-open door and said, 'What's wrong? What the hell are you doing?' I thought something bad had happened.

He pushed past me and entered my room with an unopened bottle of champagne (which he'd obviously swiped from the open bar) under his arm. Survival instinct set in. I remained standing at the open doorway, and I spoke as loudly as I could, in the hope I'd wake someone else. 'Come on, leave my room. Everyone's gone to bed.'

He didn't budge and instead replied, 'Yes. You and I are going to bed.'

The feeling of being unsafe turned to raw fear.

Just as I was about to attempt to flee, a fellow male executive appeared. My strategy had worked. He was in the room next to me and had heard the raised voices. He told me afterwards that the look of horror and fear in my eyes told him straightaway that this was serious. The perpetrator towered over him as well and would have easily overpowered him in a physical battle, so I think my rescuer's survival instincts also kicked in, realising that removing him physically from my room might not be successful. He put his arm around the aggressor in a blokey, friendly way and coaxed him out by saying, 'Come on mate, off to bed, you've had too much to drink.'

Totally rattled, I couldn't sleep. I used all my strength to move the desk across the room and up against the door.

The next morning my rescuer and I went for a walk at morning tea and he asked me, 'Did you get an apology?'

'No.'

'He's probably claiming he can't remember it anyway.'

Apart from sharing the horror of the experience with close family and friends, I never filed a formal complaint or did anything to report the man.

Some months later, a message was passed to me by another male colleague from a woman who worked interstate, an employee in her twenties, who was several levels down from me in the organisation. She had been sexually approached by this same man at a company function, which others witnessed. Distraught, she had asked her male colleague and friend who, like me, was based in the Melbourne head office, to 'tell Julia … she's one I trust'.

I'm sure the fact that I was one of the few female senior executives contributed to that trust.

This was different to my personal case. My professional obligation and duty of care as a senior executive lawyer spurred me to action it as best I could at the most senior level.

You may ask why I didn't report my own incident. At that time, I was only analysing this situation as it affected me personally – as a woman, not as a lawyer or executive director. I was simply trusting my gut instinct. My survival instinct. Even though I had an eyewitness, I didn't think I would be believed. After all, I'd been drinking and having fun too. And as much as the perpetrator and I were both executives, he was more senior, and an expat on a temporary assignment. He had connections higher in the echelons of the global giant than me or my rescuer, and he would often brag, 'They'll never let go of me or give me a termination package … I'm too expensive.' He was right.

A few days after I'd taken action on behalf of the junior employee, I was advised that the matter had been 'dealt with' and was addressed 'appropriately'. He was apparently 'spoken to' and given a warning, and reassurances were given that he 'won't do it again'. But he wasn't leaving the company.

A warning was probably a badge of honour for him. The 'word' was that, when working overseas, he'd received warnings about misconduct before. Probably other women in the organisation had been told he wouldn't do it again.

After my own incident, I'd had an enduring sense of anxiety and many sleepless nights as I kept churning over in my mind what could have happened, had it not been for my other colleague stepping in. I also hadn't felt that there was anyone who could confidentially handle it for me without the aggressor finding out – and that reprisals and retribution would follow. It turned out that in that case that my instinct was right again.

The man found out that I was one of the sources in reporting the other incident involving the junior employee. He then commenced an almost imperceptible, pervasive and systemic undermining of my professional standing in the organisation. He was making sure that would be my primary penalty for speaking up. It was coupled with my having to work alongside him. I studiously maintained a 'no eye-contact rule' – as much as was humanly possible when you work with someone. One night I was working back late at the office and I heard his booming voice talking on the phone. I realised that we were the only two executives left in the office. I hurriedly packed up and ran to the car park, got in my car and locked the door.

*

When the #MeToo movement took hold, it didn't take long for pushback or 'reservations' to emerge – from both men and women. Some labelled it a witch hunt against men. Some complained that the #MeToo movement suppresses seduction and harmless flirting – including a group of one hundred women of influence in France who objected to the movement on terms of 'sexual freedom'.

Relationships are complex, and in the workplace even more so. Of course, many men and women engage in flirty behaviour and exchanges in the workplace – often, they are wanted attentions and consensual relationships. The ABC Australia Talks national survey of more than 54,000 Australians reveals that, since 2010, more people meet their partner online than anywhere else, but meeting their partner at work is still ranked third (after mutual friend introductions). I met the great love of my life, my husband of twenty-eight years, at work (in a lift in the office building of our mutual employer) – as did many more people my age before connecting online was 'a thing'.

But the #MeToo movement didn't emerge because of people meeting and then perhaps breaking up with their partners at work – the movement is not an attack on love, romance, marriage, adultery or sex and singles. It is about power. Abuses of power. And power imbalances. These power imbalances can render workplace cultures toxic and unsafe, particularly for young women.

Many women engage in flirtation because they instinctively don't want to upset the man in question, especially so if he's a powerful man, or there is a power disparity. Where it gets out of control is when the person in power abuses that position – when their sense of entitlement eclipses any respect, and when a line is crossed into sexual harassment, unwanted sexual advances or touching, sexual assault or rape.

Even consensual relationships become complicated when there is a power disparity, whether they are happily ever after, on again off again, an extramarital romance or acrimonious break-up. And in all these cases, a couple of things usually stay the same: the person in the position of power is usually a man, and if things end in tears, the one who cops damage to their reputation, the loser in this equation of two, will almost certainly be the woman.

This power imbalance was crystal clear in the 2020 independent investigation findings that High Court Justice Dyson Heydon sexually harassed six young female associates. Heydon's status as one of the most powerful men in the country – not to mention the law itself, which excluded judges and MPs from the Sex Discrimination Act – had protected him from any accountability.

One week after the Heydon story broke, we learned of another disturbing story, this time from the corporate world. At a town hall meeting for AMP employees, the new chief executive Boe Pahari was asked directly to explain how he could guarantee an appropriate environment for the firm's diverse workforce, following revelations he'd been promoted to the top role after settling a sexual harassment claim with a financial penalty. A darkly familiar pattern had followed: the woman involved had left the company, while the perpetrator was promoted.

Promoting or protecting perpetrators is not a new phenomenon. I know of more incidents than I could ever list here of women who have encountered bad behaviour – often from men who already have a 'reputation' or from men very high up in power structures – and find that their organisation is slow to respond appropriately, if they respond at all. If action is taken, the woman's professional standing is often called into question, she is regarded as a troublemaker, or she is portrayed as the sexually promiscuous one. 'She threw herself at him. She was drunk. She wears flimsy clothes. She sleeps around. She's a slut. She asked for it.'

Disturbingly, AMP Capital Chairman John Fraser, a powerful financial figure, had told a podcast in 2020, 'I would just make sure that when I was at [work] functions, I would be with people I trusted to make sure that if anybody made false allegations against me or the people I was with, I would have someone to provide contrary evidence.'

Sadly, this is a reflection of a commonly held view that women have an ulterior motive for making these things up. It's been proven time and again that, as Dr Julia Baird puts it, 'There are so very few false allegations. The greater question is – what happens to the far more numerous real, substantial ones – those found to be true? Are the men given a quick slap then a big promotion, while the women quietly exit, distressed?'

There are countless women out there who are the holders of secrets and non-disclosure agreements that guarantee their silence on these matters.

Virginia Trioli reflected on our silence: 'We keep men's secrets. We hesitate to reveal our abuse and our shame. We sometimes go to the police. But more often we don't. We feel unable to speak out, we feel unsafe about speaking out. We can be punished for speaking out in ways that mirror our abuse.'

In essence, this means that for many women in any sector, the workplace is not somewhere they can feel safe.

*

Colloquially referred to as 'the House' by its daily occupants, our federal parliament is perhaps the most unsafe house in Australia. The building houses the centre of our country's power – but the power disparity between the men and women within it is as imposing as the building itself is on the landscape of our capital.

It's a place where sexism and misogyny are rife. It's a place where women have suffered against a backdrop of fear and silence. They have seen what happens to women who have elected to speak up about the many men more powerful than them.

The design of our political system and sheer scale of Parliament

House – where all MPs have private offices, usually containing a stacked mini bar fridge – means you don't have to wait for the office Christmas party, offsite work function or even fortnightly Friday night drinks. But banning alcohol or implementing drug and alcohol testing in Parliament House, which should happen sooner rather than later, is just one housekeeping item.

The real problem is complicated and deeply embedded in the endemic culture. The sexism and misogyny is so pervasive and constant that many people are blind to inappropriate behaviour when it is actually happening. I've witnessed, heard about and personally experienced enough to comfortably believe that some form of casual sexism, sexual harassment, unwelcome sexual advance or sexual assault happens in our Parliament House every single sitting day, and night.

It doesn't even have to happen in the privacy of the individual MP offices. It happens in the restaurants, pubs, hotels and streets of Canberra. It doesn't need the context of alcohol, partying or after-hours social events. It happens during the daily grind of a workday – in the corridors and stairwells. In business, we've all heard that 'what happens at the conference stays at the conference' and, similarly, in Canberra the unofficial line is 'what happens in Canberra stays in Canberra'.

I know of a staffer who was walking along the corridor to go to a meeting in another office. An MP who was walking behind her quickened his pace to catch up to her and said, 'Those pants you're wearing would look great on my wife,' whereupon he put his hand on the inside of them, pulled them out a few inches from her waist and said, 'What brand are they?' He seemed to think mentioning his wife made it all okay.

Once when passing a middle-aged, married male MP in the corridor, I briefly stopped to talk and he introduced me to a new young staff member who was standing next to him. As he introduced her, he sleazily ran his hand up and down her back. She physically flinched as she politely said hello to me.

The young woman and I looked at each other and I was certain her eyes were saying, *Please don't say anything.* Granted that could have been the wrong interpretation on my part. But she probably knew what I knew: that if I spoke up then and there, I would put her in an embarrassing situation where she had to insist everything was fine, and if I followed up, I knew the systems and processes bizarrely would have made it worse for the young woman. The main way it would ultimately be dealt with would be to sweep it under the carpet and get it out of the way – and also likely get the young woman 'out of the way'. There is literally nowhere for these women to go. Nowhere they can feel safe. Nowhere their story can be confidential.

So, there I was, in practical terms as powerless as she was. And yet I was a member of parliament, more senior, a lawyer, a woman who knew what needed to be done in this situation (and would have done so if the exact same scenario had happened in a corporate context), but one who also knew that the structures for addressing these situations are simply non-existent in these corridors of power.

When I called out the entrenched anti-woman culture within the coalition in 2018, Prime Minister Scott Morrison called for an 'internal review' into workplace misconduct. Other women MPs who'd called out the behaviour at the same time as I did – but who were intending to stay in the party – backed down, repeating their new leader's patriarchal wisdom that these matters were all best handled 'internally'. In fact, both major parties swiftly let it be known that they each had their own 'internal processes' for this situation – which looked very similar, apart from the party badges. The bipartisan approach was really a form of collusion between the duopoly of power. It was very unclear as to how that internal review progressed. I was curious that I was certainly not asked any questions for this review – I'm guessing they wouldn't have liked the answers.

At the time of my calling out the anti-woman culture, many women came forward and spoke to me. Many told me that they trusted me to keep their confidence. Many also expressed that, because I'm a woman with similar lived experience, they trusted I would believe them. I think some just wanted a kind of cathartic reassurance that it was 'not just them'. And for others, they recognised I was in a position of power where they thought I could 'do something'. These women were one of the reasons for my inspiration to continue in politics.

One was a young woman whose voice started breaking when she began to tell me a story that had happened many years earlier, when she was an intern for a senior MP. I was told that at the end of one of her first days on the job, they'd had drinks in his office, and he'd invited a couple of other male MPs. The things they were saying were enough to make her think they were going to lock the door (all MPs offices have a door with an internal lock). She felt she had to get out, as she felt unsafe from pending sexual assault. She made up some excuse the next day about being sick and never went back. Not surprisingly, she pursued a career outside of politics.

One night in Canberra, I was lying awake until the early hours. I couldn't sleep. Churning over and over in my mind were the implications of an incident that had happened only a few hours earlier. The incident was minor compared to many of my past experiences. An incident that, being a corporate lawyer, I knew would only classify as 'an unwelcome sexual advance' – if that.

The manoeuvre itself was the 'hand-on-knee' manoeuvre that may sound familiar. It's not the first time I'd experienced it – it's not even the first time it's appeared in this book.

I'd only been an MP for around a year at the time, and this was my first experience of hanging around the House into the night for the sole purpose of waiting for the bells to ring for a vote. It was getting late and all the coalition MPs were invited to the prime minister's wing for drinks and snacks. A more seasoned MP explained to me it was a kind of 'grown-ups roll call' to make sure we all actually turned up for the vote – an imperative with a one-seat majority. It's a sad testament to the quality of some of the MPs in our government that the only way to ensure they show up to an important lawmaking vote is to get them together in one room with the lure of alcohol and food and keep a watchful eye on them to make sure they don't leave, fall asleep, or worse get so drunk in their own office that they pass out and miss the vote (this had happened before). The longer we had to wait, the more alcohol was consumed.

I was seated on a couch making conversation with a female MP seated on my left. After a while, a male minister came over and sat down on my right. I turned to acknowledge him and flinched slightly at the smell of alcohol on his breath when he asked, not really expecting an answer, 'How are you, Julia?' Within seconds this was followed by the hand-on-knee manoeuvre. It was more than fleeting, and certainly not accidental. His hand landed just above my knee and edged slowly and deliberately to my inner thigh and then further up my leg. The only saving grace was that this time I was wearing suit pants, not a skirt and bare legs. For a minister to do this in the prime minister's wing, which was full of coalition MPs, he had to be astoundingly brazen. I found it unbelievable. And I momentarily froze.

Without pausing, the minister then got up from the couch and went over to say something to some people a couple of metres from where I was sitting. His body language indicated he was clearly intending to go back to his original seat, as if his manoeuvre were some kind of signal to gauge my interest – to see if I would stay there and wait for him. I didn't. Despite my momentary state of shock, I had the instinctive wherewithal to leave my seat and walk over to the food and drinks table to stand beside another female MP. I whispered something along the lines of, 'Can you stay ... he made a move on me ... talk to me.' When he came over to try to interrupt us, I moved away again.

The whole incident was over in a short period. After the vote came down (in the early hours of the morning), I went back to my office, collected my things, left the House and went to my hotel. I know that far worse has happened to millions of women, including myself, in terms of unwelcome attention or inappropriate touching. In some ways I saw it as a transient and trivial incident and put it down to a ridiculous drunken moment by an entitled narcissist, as a kind of 'power' move. I also knew that even if I tried to manage it myself, and spoke to him directly – which would have usually been my first line of action in this situation – he would do nothing more than deny it and make my working life difficult.

But there's no denying the situation was unique: that a senior MP, a cabinet minister, had felt so confident to act this way within the walls of Parliament House, in the prime minister's wing – and he had 'gold-class' plausible deniability credentials.

What kept me awake was more the thought of what he might have done or could do to other women. Younger women, less senior women. Women where there is a significant power disparity, whose job depended on men in power. Staffers or press gallery journalists.

I kept thinking to myself over and over, *If he was prepared to do that to me – a fifty-something, corporate lawyer MP – in that room, what must he do to these women he has real power over?*

The 2020 *Four Corners* 'Inside the Canberra Bubble' exposed the inappropriate conduct of two senior government cabinet ministers, and a culture that can be toxic for women. The government had attempted to block the story before it aired. Louise Milligan, the Walkley-award-winning forensic investigative reporter, likened the Morrison Government's siege mentality and use of institutional power against the national broadcaster to the behaviour of the Catholic Church when confronted with allegations of child abuse. 'It was fascinating in the lead-up to the story how the forces corralled to try and shut it down.'

If that institutional power was directed without hesitation at the behemoth that is the country's national broadcaster for calling out bad behaviour, it doesn't take much to imagine how swiftly and deliberately the force of that institutional power might be used to try to mute an individual. Especially an individual with little power.

A young government staffer, Brittany Higgins, alleged she was raped in a minister's office in March 2019. These allegations go off the scale of workplace misconduct. This is an allegation of rape. A crime that is only one down from murder and manslaughter, has allegedly happened in what is meant to be the most tightly secure building in the country. Higgins told her harrowing story publicly in early 2021, two years after the alleged rape occurred.

The response, both when Higgins first alleged the rape to the powers that be (two months before the 2019 election) and then to the public, was shocking in and of itself. This painful experience for this woman was compounded by the Morrison Government's incompetence, mismanagement and lack of accountability and humanity. It became clear that dozens of people had known, but Morrison maintained that he didn't know about it until the day the story broke. He started bringing up his old favourite 'internal reviews'. Journalist Peter Hartcher saw through this, as many did: the 'time-honoured "internal review" ... Guaranteed to come to no difficult conclusions and fade away like all the others. This is the "business as usual" reflex, suppression disguised as action.'

Added to this was Morrison's over-familiarity, referring to Higgins only as 'Brittany', infantilising her, and suggesting she was of weak emotional disposition. This had an eerily familiar ring to it. In a statement released forty-eight hours after the story broke, Higgins said what I suspect most women in the country were feeling for her: 'The continued victim-blaming rhetoric by the prime minister is personally very distressing to me and countless other survivors.'

Brittany Higgins's courage and personal power in the most dire of circumstances is extraordinary. Disturbingly, it was the image of Scott Morrison standing next to Australian of the Year Grace Tame, a survivor of sexual assault who has campaigned for #LetHerSpeak, that Higgins says made her speak out. 'I was sick to my stomach,' she said. 'He's standing next to a woman who has campaigned for #LetHerSpeak and yet in my mind his government was complicit in silencing me. It was a betrayal. It was a lie.'

To see a young woman have to withstand this treatment after telling the most horrendous account of her experience – and to know that there are countless other women seeing in real time what the consequences are of calling out bad behaviour within this government – made me also feel 'sick to my stomach', with sadness and with anger. But the government persisted with, as Jenna Price called it, 'emotional and mental abuse of the very highest order. Control. Deny. Demean. Degrade.'

It was then revealed that a woman who had since taken her own life made allegations of rape in 1988 against Christian Porter – one of the two ministers who was at the centre of the *Four Corners* investigation. Porter has strenuously denied the allegations of rape, initiated defamation proceedings against the ABC and Louise Milligan, and stepped back from his duties as attorney-general. Morrison has consistently rejected calls from across Australia and from the late woman's family for an independent inquiry.

Often a public story can trigger memories of a similar incident. Many women across the country were, like me, triggered by the reporting of these recent issues paired with the government's dismissive response. It sparked a response that engulfed the country and a movement that started under the title March4Justice – a movement against sexism, misogyny and gendered violence against women. Tens of thousands of men and women attended rallies in forty locations, including regional areas, country towns and capital cities. Poignantly, the marches were held almost a hundred years to the day after the first woman was elected to an Australian parliament (Edith Cowan in WA). Brittany Higgins attended and spoke at the rally in Canberra.

The organisers had asked me to speak at the Melbourne rally. Feeling nervous but resolute, I stood on the stage and opened my speech: 'When I was asked to speak here today, I said no. I was frightened. I was scared. I've seen what those in our centre of power will do if you speak up. They try to silence you. They create fear. They paint a picture or narrative about you in the media of someone you're not. They issue legal proceedings. And all of that creates the threats and abuse. What changed my mind to speak up today was because of you. All of you.' And I gestured my arms out to the crowd.

In response, the ten-thousand-strong crowd blanketing the CBD of my hometown collectively roared their support with a warmth and love and passion. It is a moment I shall treasure for the rest of my life.

In what has been described by Peter Hartcher as 'a death spiral', Morrison's mismanagement and lack of accountability seemed to reinforce rather than address the toxic anti-women workplace culture. Morrison said it was a triumph for the March4Justice protesters that they weren't 'met with bullets'. He asked women to stand with him, even though, when thousands marched in the streets in solidarity advocating for the safety of women – many of who have had their own safety or security away from them or know someone who has – he wouldn't walk a few hundred metres to stand with *them* and listen. He constantly undermined his intended message through partisan weaponry, references to 'glass houses', and telling media to 'be careful' before asking questions, effectively telling the opposition, media and others to stay silent because 'we have dirt on you'.

Granted, there was swift action taken against an alleged masturbatory act on a female MP's desk, and another MP was persuaded not to run at the next election after harassing his constituents and taking a photograph of a woman's underwear. But these actions only occurred after these matters became public.

In a predictably reactive and cosmetic response to the 'women problem', Morrison reshuffled his cabinet. He put more women in roles that were largely a subset of the minister for women's role, creating a 'taskforce', the membership for which required having the word 'women' in the letterhead for their newly appointed titles. As Jane Caro said on *The Drum*, it was 'pushing the women's business to the women – here you are ladies, you can look after this messy stuff ...' Grace Tame said 'We need to be careful not to be naively misled by actions that are quite calculated distractions posing as solutions.'

At one point Morrison accidentally called the minister for women (who had been largely invisible during this whole torrid time), the 'prime minister for women'. Perhaps he is only really comfortable leading men?

In every other sector I've worked with or alongside, there is an infrastructure of resources or services that ensure these matters are, in the main, managed appropriately. They are non-existent in politics. There is one thing that gets in the way of an internal investigation of workplace misconduct in politics: internal politics. Reviews make great content for media announcements but are too often a substitute for real change. As we've seen, they can be shelved, gagged, forgotten or hardly implemented. Morrison has been aptly described by his predecessor Malcolm Turnbull as a 'control freak'. His strong penchant for the internal review is likely for one reason and one reason only – he can control it.

Even characterising reviews as 'independent' offers little hope, as they depend on the government to implement them. Look at the fate of the Australian Human Rights Commission's Respect@Work report: it languished, unread, and resurfaced only as a consequence of pressure and advocacy demanding the government implement it. Once again we received a 'bells and whistles announcement', but the government's plan falls significantly short of committing to constructively implementing the recommendations, with many of them just being 'noted'.

Even though bullying and sexual harassment are often intertwined, men don't need to be sleazy or a sexual harasser to be a bully. In politics and elsewhere, if men in power find that a woman's silence can't be bought or imposed through fear, they'll do whatever they can to make sure that people don't believe the woman.

This is when the media often gets weaponised. The power of men in politics is compounded by their relationships with their favourite journalists (particularly inside Rupert Murdoch's monopoly). The politicians feed the press the narrative they want to create. A woman will be cast as emotionally weak or mentally unstable, confused, a liar, a troublemaker, the bitch, the witch, the flirt or the slut. The old 'he said, she said' line will be brought out to cast doubt on that 'bloody woman'. All to communicate one clear message, the most brutal blow: women cannot be believed.

It's hardly a surprise that the situation in Australia made international headlines, with the front page of *The New York Times* reporting that Parliament House was a 'sexist backwater' and, as I was quoted, 'the most unsafe workplace' in the country.

Brittany Higgins, Grace Tame and Chanel Contos (who has collected accounts of young women harassed and abused in schools) are all creating a tremendous voice for those who were previously not heard, let alone listened to. Annabel Crabb commented, 'This new eruption of power is occurring outside [the prime minister's] control and it's not going away ... It can create extremely uncomfortable conditions ... It can also create opportunity. There is always opportunity, when power shifts.'

In my crisis management experience, the oft-quoted wisdom from Winston Churchill is 'never waste a good crisis'. Not only has Morrison wasted this opportunity by not listening to these women's voices, but his response has embedded this as one of the worst periods in political history for women in Australia.

*

Women who have named names in the past are rightly lauded as brave and courageous. By speaking out, they have often made it better for others and carved a path for them – but at what cost to these women as individuals? The countless women who have not spoken up are no less brave. Rather, they have just made a different assessment of the very real potential consequences, and they may not have the choice of leaving their job and compromising their career options.

We cannot continue to put this burden on women and to say they must always and rigorously 'call it out', when calling it out could backfire on the women who do so, forcing them to deal with the collateral damage. That's the harsh reality. As Julia Gillard put it, to call out it out or not is the 'debate of our time' and there is 'no right answer'. It's disturbing and short-sighted when people categorically say women should call it out, and pressure them to do so. Often the consequences – to their personal circumstances, their livelihood, their career – can be more traumatic than the experience itself.

Many will want me to name the MPs in these stories. But I don't think I'm different to other women who don't go public with certain details such as names, fearing the backlash (which can be particularly acute in workplace misconduct matters of a sexual nature) and emotional harm – to myself and my loved ones. In some cases, the easier option would have been to hit the delete button on some of the stories altogether, to avoid further questions and speculation. But they're important stories to tell. I don't want to reduce a complex and vexed issue to individuals, and I want to demonstrate the breadth and extent of the toxic culture that fosters fear and creates silence.

In any event, we have seen various MPs named for bad behaviour of late, and there is no sight of any leadership or accountability. As Leigh Sales asked of the deputy leader and treasurer, 'How good does it feel to be a minister in the Morrison Government, knowing that no matter what questions arise over your conduct your job is safe?'

The 'burden' to address these situations should remain on organisations and leaders – they need to put systems in place and make the right calls about the perpetrators. But the solution will not be to rely on the 'internal review' or summits or talkfests. Rather effective implementation of real actions.

Despite Morrison (a career politician) stating that there are 'other houses that need to be fixed up', my corporate experience informs me differently about other workplace cultures which, while not perfect, are much better than that of Parliament House. But there's still more to do in other sectors. The AMP case and the Dyson Heydon case can't be dismissed as high profile 'bad apples'. From the small to medium workplaces to the large powerful organisations, you can encounter this behaviour in any sector, at any stage, at any time, on every rung of that career ladder towards leadership.

The Australian Human Rights Commission's 2018 national survey on sexual harassment in Australian workplaces showed that one in three people had experienced sexual harassment in the workplace. Women and young people are at the highest risk. Situations associated with higher prevalence rates include hierarchical workplaces, male-dominated workplaces and client-facing roles. My experiences of sexual harassment as a young female lawyer working in private practice and in the courts sadly remain relevant: in a recent Review of Sexual Harassment in Victorian Courts it was found that 61 per cent of women and 12 per cent of men had experienced sexual harassment in a legal workplace.

One of the most disturbing elements of this is that it acts as a deterrent to emerging or future women leaders.

We can and must stop it. How?

In some cases, there can be success with specific policies and structures set up within and across organisations.

Having spent most of my career in the manufacturing sector, I saw the transformative changes from occupational health and safety legislation – and this was because of the high level of accountability attributed to the leaders of the businesses in the event of a breach. Slowly but surely, the number of safety breaches reduced across the sector. And slowly but surely, safety came to include psychological safety.

James Fazzino, chairman of Manufacturing Australia and former CEO of Incitec Pivot, has said that boards and executives should deal with and manage sexual harassment complaints 'with the same level of urgency and transparency as they did with occupational health and safety'.

The Champions of Change Coalition is a group of senior corporate leaders – mainly men, since it's mainly men who are still in power. Following the spate of recent high-profile cases of sexual misconduct, they released a report calling for a complete overhaul of how companies identify and investigate sexual harassment cases. They also called for companies to better educate staff, and to put an end to non-disclosure agreements that serve to silence the victims. Many of Australia's leading businesses have signed the Diversity Council Australia #IStandForRespect pledge to stamp out sexual harassment in the workplace.

Many companies now have a policy to address the issues office relationships can cause when there is a power disparity. This underpins why Malcolm Turnbull introduced revised Ministerial Standards, which included what was dubbed the 'bonk ban', preventing ministers from having sexual relations with their staff. There was mixed commentary at the time about 'gross overreach' or being the 'morality police', as there was when the Australian Football League sacked two executives for having consensual extramarital affairs with younger women in the workplace.

These codes seek to spell out executive accountability and influence employees to live the values of the organisation, but they aren't the be all and end all and are often difficult to enforce. These situations put an accountability on both the individuals involved. No matter how consensual, any workplace relationships should trigger a warning in the personal code of the individuals concerned. And where there's a significant power disparity, there's a higher onus on the more senior person to do the right thing.

Most importantly, all workplaces should have an independent investigative whistle-blower system. It should be embraced in federal law. And the lawmakers should ensure it applies to themselves as well.

But in the end, the problem goes deeper than any policy or code, housekeeping matters or even an external reporting system. The burden should not be on the women to speak up – rather it should be on those in power to make the decisions to change the structures, and its culture. Culture can only be changed from the decisions made (which sometimes include 'tough calls') and the values demonstrated by those at the top. As it is at the moment, most of those people in power are men.

Kate Jenkins, Australian Sex Discrimination Commissioner, said in regard to the Dyson Heydon case, 'The key driver of sexual harassment is power, not sex, and gender inequality is still the most significant power disparity driving sexual harassment.'

Jenkins also recognised in an interview that 'It is absolutely no coincidence that this is a High Court which for the first time has gender balance, has three women ... the Chief Justice is a woman. For sexual harassment, we've heard across the board that if people come forward, gender-balanced leadership teams are the best environments for reduced sexual harassment.' They are the places where complaints are fully addressed and questions heard and answered. And believed. 'With male dominated leaders, they tend to be more questioning about if it's genuine …'

In the midst of the AMP media storm, the only woman in the room in the leadership team was Helen Livesey. She said in a team meeting held online, 'It's actually really difficult to be the only woman on the senior leadership team and to be the person who needs to front this, but as I said, it actually makes me more determined.'

Gender-equal leadership teams are not the total panacea. But rather an urgent imperative. If the High Court can get there, surely the corporate world and our body politic can. They are proven to make a difference – to the culture, the dialogue, the collective expectations of conduct. Most importantly, as the Australian Human Rights Commission Respect@Work report has shown definitively, women are more inclined to speak to other women leaders, with whom they feel safe and believed. And women are even more likely to be believed by another woman in power if that woman is a member of a gender-equal team. 'Their accounts of their experiences at the time have been believed' was a truly powerful statement made by Chief Justice Susan Kiefel when announcing the outcome of the Heydon investigation, and a statement that I'm sure resonated with millions of women.

Leaders often say they have 'zero tolerance' for workplace misconduct. But we're at risk of these two powerful words becoming cliché and meaningless. What's needed is 'zero tolerance of no accountability' for these issues. Leaders of organisations and governments operate at their peril, and not in the interests of their people, if they only assess individual incidents and not a pattern of behaviour, and if they continue to nurture a culture of silence and fear.

And if they don't believe the women.

Chapter 9

In leaders we trust

Standing on a stage in front of a four-hundred-plus audience of employees, a senior executive held up a balloon. He asked his large audience to imagine this balloon represented the company's reputation, which was founded on the core value of trust. He then dramatically popped it. 'Break that trust, and everything goes.'

In any career, the more senior you get and the more accountability you acquire, the higher the highs, and the more challenging the lows. But no matter whether you're a prime minister or political staffer, a CEO or the junior manager of a small division, you're still a leader. What makes you a leader isn't a title. It is the trust and respect of your team.

Leaders define the culture, and therefore should be held to a higher standard, where accountability is a minimum expectation. They embody the metaphorical 'trust balloon', and they are responsible for keeping it intact.

Having worked in the legal and corporate world for over twenty-five years, in matrix organisations across multiple business functions, I've had many experiences as a team member and a team leader. Because of the nature of my roles, my solid reporting lines were largely to the senior executives based overseas in the international parent company, with dotted lines to the local CEOs and regional VPs, so I was often seen as the 'Switzerland' on the leadership team. Consequently, I often became the trusted confidant of these various senior leaders – my 'dotted line bosses' as well as my peers. I've seen CEOs and VPs come and go, which has enabled me to observe a generous sample of the good and the great leaders.

I've also seen the bad and the ugly. But in the businesses for which I've worked, if a leader breached the team's trust or displayed a pattern of behaviour that was contrary to the organisation's values, they would generally be either fired, 'managed out' of their job, seriously counselled, or stood aside so that an independent investigation could take place. This was the case for leaders of either gender – although if a man had to 'performance manage' a direct report or employee who was not meeting job expectations, he would be seen as strong or assertive, whereas in the same situation a woman ran the risk of being labelled a bully or a bitch.

Given my governance and compliance role at a senior level, I provided advice and counsel in relation to many of these situations. And I saw that it was only when a leader, either their boss or themselves, demonstrated accountability and took appropriate action, that there would be a recalibration towards or back to a healthy workplace culture.

Good and great leaders will consistently demonstrate high accountability for not only the successes of their teams and the individuals in those teams, but also for the failures. It's all about the power of the team. No matter the sector, leaders who define their purpose and power as being able to get the best out of those who work with them and for them, in turn, always get the best outcomes. Every business leader I know, every business text or conference you will ever go to, will tell you that teamwork delivers success.

On the opposite end of the spectrum is abuse of power, when positional power is used to diminish people, undermine them, create fear or impose silence. It's usually driven by the person in power's own individual motives. Abuse of power at work is often referred to as 'workplace coercive control' – defined as 'an abusive strategy targeted at a specific person that limits that person's autonomy, sense of wellbeing and ability to succeed at work'.

Building relationships with people is a powerful ingredient in leadership. Your interactions with people, whether they seem negative and toxic or brilliant and positive, all build character and leadership skills in ways that should never be underestimated. Establishing personal relationships with your team members, as individuals and as a team, is an essential for any leader. Theodore Roosevelt's famous lengthy quotation about the arena ('The credit belongs to the man [or woman!] who is actually in the arena, whose face is marred by dust and sweat and blood ... who does actually strive to do the deeds ... who spends himself [or herself] in a worthy cause') is often used to describe what great leadership represents. But the man or woman in the arena doesn't get to be in the arena without the support of those around them. This applies in any arena – not just in the sporting one.

I'm sure many believe, like I did, that on the 'inside' a government party operates like any good business workplace culture that has issues from time to time. But from the moment I entered politics through the pathway of a major party, I found an entirely different world to anything I had experienced before – a world where distrust, disrespect and irrational behaviour are brazenly substituted for trust, respect and collaboration. A world where logic and facts are often displaced by irrational argument and PR message points. Where experience and expertise are often rejected, ignored and clouded by envy and prejudice. Where higher standards are rarely imposed, in particular for male leaders. Where things often happen for power alone, rather than purpose. The antithesis of a team.

In other sectors, a big focus is placed on induction, governance and ethics training, and leadership development. A huge part of my life has been training employees in governance, laws and workplace policies and codes of conduct, from the most senior CEOs to people on the factory floor. Yet in our federal parliament this sort of training and these structures are completely non-existent. Both the major parties have historically created codes of conduct, but they are voluntary and internal, generally rendered unenforceable, forgotten about and completely ineffective. 'Pollies' school' for new members just covers what I call the housekeeping factors. Many parliamentarians manage their office and team with absolutely no people-management experience. And it shows.

It goes without saying at this point that most of the people in positions of power in Australia's political duopoly are men. The men I will talk about in this chapter have leadership positions that don't just have influence over a workplace – they impact a whole country. Whether you have positional power or not, the most satisfying and rewarding power is power that enables you to make a difference and give your voice to others. But the focus of too many of these men in politics seems to be on power plays alone.

*

During my very first sitting week in parliament, an admired and seasoned female minister gave me a short, sharp and potent induction lesson, with just three words: 'Don't. Trust. Anyone.'

Many people assume those in the opposition party are, as the word implies, your opponents, your competitors. Not so. The real enemies, the fiercest opponents are sitting on the same side as you.

The 'leadership' in federal politics, in practical terms, is fragmented and operates at different levels from local branches and state branches. The power of the federal organisation doesn't play out as a parent company would over its subsidiaries. Many of the so-called leaders of the political class are people who wouldn't survive two weeks in a good corporation. I had to feign tolerance of the branch members, 'officials' and self-proclaimed powerbrokers – the oft-quoted 'faceless men' – but I didn't feel I could trust any of them. It seemed to me that teamwork was something they could only relate to in the context of sport. They saw politics as more of a gladiator's arena than something you pursue for the public good.

Anyone in a managerial or leadership position knows that one of the advantages of being a leader is that you get to select and build your own team. In politics, it's different. Before I was elected, I was told to work with individuals recruited and employed by those same faceless men; true to the 'like recruits like' philosophy, these men were anything but team players. I approached preselection and then the election in the same way that I had any business project: with a plan and goal. But I was becoming increasingly incredulous that my accustomed 'business model', founded on trust, teamwork and respect, was ineffective in this world. I couldn't believe it when I realised that many of the actions of those around me were taken purely for the purpose of making me fail.

But it was their plan that failed.

I felt excited and relieved when, on the other side of the 2016 election campaign, I found in Malcolm Turnbull a leader with whom I shared core values and beliefs, and most importantly, someone who I could trust. With his own business career and achievements behind him, it was obvious that his 'purpose' for using his power and leadership in politics was for the bigger benefit of society. Two of his values always stood out for me – integrity, and his deep belief in equality. Not only is he a self-proclaimed feminist, but he underscored this with real action; as Anne Summers described, he 'championed women's equality and invested in a $100 million Women's Safety Package', and introduced rules and mechanisms, including the Ministerial Standards (aka the bonk ban).

On a personal level, the empathetic support he gave to me during the citizenship crisis was particularly extraordinary. Once, during a particularly intense and complex time for the government, I had to leave the parliament as my mother was involved in a terrible car accident. In the midst of our text messages on political matters of the day and just after he did a live press conference, he texted, 'How's Mum?'

But under Morrison's leadership I felt the full brunt of a culture of fear and silence, underpinned by sexism and misogyny. Those three months represented the most gut-wrenching, distressing period in my entire career. It seemed that in place of a team, the powerful forces against me in the Victorian branch of the party had merged with the most powerful forces in Canberra, led by the new prime minister. There was no trust. Zero.

One dark and rainy Melbourne Friday night in 2018, I was meant to be going to a footy game at the Melbourne Cricket Ground with my family. It was to be a special and rare family outing, a gift from my adult children to my husband, and we were all looking forward to it, but we were halfway there and I knew I wouldn't be able to concentrate on the game. Instead, I dropped off my family out the front of the ground, trying to reassure them, although they all had deeply concerned looks on their faces. 'At least we won't have to find a car parking space,' I joked. I did a

U-turn and started the drive back home.

Recent events were spinning in my head. The gaslighting, abuse and threats, the coercion, the people who 'knew where I lived'. I'd spent that day captive in my own home, with photographers and the Australian Federal Police parked outside my house – who, in their different roles, were both fuelling and protecting me from the attacks and abuse. One of the photographers had tried to follow us on the way to the football.

As I drove home, alone, the headlights from the intense traffic distorting my vision and the windscreen wipers going frantically because of the heavy rain, my phone rang. The caller's tone was bullying, short and swift and coldly calculating.

I was rattled. As I pulled into our driveway, my phone was pinging with concerned text messages from my family, making sure I'd got home safely. I turned the ignition off and, as I hurriedly got out of my car, saw dark shadows appearing near the front gate. For about thirty seconds, which felt like thirty minutes, I felt real fear. I realised at that very point in time that I was up against the most powerful forces in the land. And there seemed no escape. I was the whistle blower and they wanted me gone. There was no one I could trust.

I fumbled putting my keys into the front door. And somewhere, somehow, in this moment I found a new energy, determination and strength. As I breathed a deep sigh and leant against the closed door, standing inside the safety of my home, I thought to myself, *Fuck them, I could get out – on my own terms.*

*

Rewind to only a few weeks prior, and in the days before the final strike against Malcolm Turnbull, Parliament House was engulfed by, as Turnbull himself said, 'a form of madness'.

'Scott Morrison' – the name flashed up on my phone. He asked, with an almost presumptuous tone, whether he had my support 'in the event there's a challenge'. I finally said I would vote for him, but despondently expressed my utter disbelief at what was happening.

He told me, 'You are exactly the sort of woman we need in the party.'

Whatever that meant, I knew that I was not Scott Morrison's sort of woman. I was a backbencher (low power) and a professional career woman (not a traditional homemaker), who was showing great potential to be an out-of-control troublemaker. An MP who had worked with Morrison longer than I read my mind when he took over the leadership; she said, 'He doesn't really like or understand women like you or me, women who have worked in a profession and who have children.'

I *was* the sort of woman, and I'm told the only woman, who voted for another woman to be our leader.

Soon after my phone call with Morrison, the rumour going around that Julie Bishop would be running was formally confirmed by Bishop. As one of my fellow Julie Bishop voters rightly said, 'This is our lifeline.' One friend asked me: 'What if Julie loses by one vote to Dutton … you'll be responsible for giving Australia Dutton as PM.' But if Dutton had been elected prime minister, I was resolute that I would have stood up in the party room and quit, triggering a by-election. Others said they would do the same.

I called Morrison back and told him I wouldn't be voting for him. The deep sigh on the other end of the phone was a mix of frustration and anger. My resolute tone didn't stop him from asking whether there was anything he could do to change my mind. And it obviously didn't stop him from sending in 'his boys'. Because minutes later, Morrison's man in the office opposite me – a backbencher and Morrison's long-time flatmate, with whom I'd only ever exchanged polite small talk – walked across to my office to tell my staff he wanted to 'catch up'.

The behaviour shown by Morrison's men – and yes, they were all men – in this period displayed the greatest sense of urgency and focus I'd seen in any of them, coupled with an immature sense of excitement. Watching these men come and go from the opposite office, it seemed to me that what had been, up until then, two separate groups in the party was emerging as one. The right-wing faction (led by Peter Dutton) and the conservative, Christian, monarchist faction (led by Morrison) were becoming a monopoly. And they were all plotting, not policy making. I imagined them all huddled together inside that office, like footballers before a big grand final or at half-time, clumped together in the locker room with all that testosterone-filled fervour, 'talking tactics' and high-fiving their take-downs.

I managed to dodge this backbencher all day, but the night before the vote, he'd finally found his way into my office – with his pack. They had arrived with the air that they expected to continue their drinking and wouldn't leave, like really annoying, oppressively loud dinner guests. My staffer ordered pizza and called me into her office for a 'confidential discussion', hoping it would be a good ploy to get them out. 'And anyway, I'm not sharing this pizza with those fuckers,' she whispered to me.

Her ploy worked, but this particular MP decided to exit past my staffer's office – it seemed he'd suddenly realised he still hadn't delivered on his objective for his new captain. Centimetres from my face, pointing to me for added emphasis, and with booze amplifying his voice, he said, 'You have to vote for Scott. Don't be an idiot. Turnbull's gone. I have it directly from the very highest authority.'

'But Turnbull is the prime minister. He is the highest authority,' I said in a calm and steely tone.

He rolled his eyes as if to mock my naivete. 'No, believe me. I know. I am *very close* to the highest authority.'

His lobbying didn't succeed with me – but he must have had success elsewhere. After the leadership change, while he didn't quite move in to The Lodge with his former flatmate, he did find himself spending a lot more time there, being appointed to the prestigious role of assistant minister to the prime minister.

The weekend after the leadership coup, the new deputy leader called me, barely concealing his elation that the coup had meant a significant elevation in his career trajectory. He indicated strongly that I'd be up for an assistant ministry. 'What would you like?' he asked.

I spent that weekend issuing statements about Turnbull and Bishop, and I also issued a statement to clarify that I'd voted for Julie Bishop in the first round of voting to correct a misleading media report that indicated I had voted for Morrison. By the end of that Sunday, the deputy leader called me again: 'Scott said ... not this time.'

This wasn't a surprise to me. I hadn't voted for Morrison, I didn't owe him anything, and I couldn't be bought. The only reason I was in any way still the 'sort of woman he needed' was because I represented that one seat, that one number in the one-seat majority.

Nonetheless, I pressed on. On the Monday morning, working from home, I asked my staff to search for photos of me with the new PM and his deputy and to post them on social media with the caption 'Looking forward to working with this leadership duo to continue to deliver'. Then I went out for a brisk walk to clear my head.

As I was walking, I checked social media, and as soon as I saw that post staring back at me, my head became very clear. I knew there was no way I could be true to myself and stand alongside Morrison and campaign with him. It was at that point, standing in the park, that I made my decision that I was not going to recontest the next election. The party and the people within it had become mired in internal political entanglements, swarming with irrational views. The general behaviour I'd observed during my short tenure with the party since 2015 had been magnified during the coup – namely, the deals, the misconduct, the tactics and the treachery. I distrusted far more people in the party room than I trusted. I could no longer look most of them in the eye, let alone talk to them.

But at the time that I decided not to recontest, I was still fully intending to 'fake it' and stay under Morrison's leadership until the next election. You don't have a successful corporate career without having to 'toe the company line' from time to time, and this has to be reflected by you as a senior executive leader or company director. I saw sticking it out under Morrison as a version of what I'd done many times before in my life.

I instructed my staff to delete the post, and I told family friends and those close to me of my decision. I got the message to Morrison through his emissaries after unsuccessful attempts to speak to him directly, leaving several messages that I wanted to talk and receiving no return call. He finally called me a few days later, just hours after he'd been sworn in.

'Julia. I. Am. The. Prime. Minister,' Morrison said to me, in a Trumpesque tone, enunciating every word with a full-stop emphasis, as if I'd missed the news cycle. (I had a flashback to this in March 2021 when he said the same to a journalist and walked off during a press conference when she challenged him.)

Morrison was trying to persuade me to not announce that I wasn't recontesting my seat. An announcement so close to the coup would make them look bad. Again he tried to bring up the possibility of a ministerial appointment 'next time', but I stopped him in his tracks. 'It's not about that,' I said, firmly but politely. He suggested that he would do a media call with me in my electorate – as if my being his prop would help me, not him.

If I was going to make an announcement, he wanted at least two months. I wanted to go straight away. 'I'm in the car about to tell my staff and finalise my media statement,' I said to him. I was – the phone call took place while I was driving to the office, with flowers, chocolates and wine as gifts for my staff.

He persisted, telling me they needed to 'plan the media roll out'. A more delayed departure announcement would have gone under the radar and could have been positioned as the cliché 'she's leaving for personal and family reasons'. That would have better suited their narrative.

I was pulling into the car park of my office by this time, and insisted I would be going live today. With a tone of someone about to lose their temper, he said, 'At least give me twenty-four hours,' to which I grudgingly relented.

Just before I posted my statement on social media on 29 August 2018, I sent this message to Morrison (and his deputy):

> Getting rid of MT and Julie in the way it happened was the last straw for me. [It was] underpinned by relentless bullying, trickery, intimidation and media leaks both last week and throughout my term … Almost as soon as I made that post about looking forward to working with you both, the great 'leadership duo', I almost immediately knew I couldn't go ahead … because of what's happened. I've had 25 years in the corporate world where loyalty and teamwork are paramount for success. The last brutal blow last week told me that teamwork is just not possible in politics …

Morrison called me soon after I posted the statement, clearly annoyed I'd issued it two hours earlier than the agreed twenty-four. I had only done so because the story was starting to leak – likely through the PMO (aka the prime minister's office). Morrison suggested he would come to my electorate to do a media conference with me standing alongside him. I couldn't think of anything worse. I politely declined. In any event, I was exhausted and planned to get away for a short break. He requested I not do any follow-up media appearances or interviews. I agreed. That was a big mistake. It gave them free rein to begin their campaign. Against me.

In the statement, I made reference to the poor treatment of women I'd 'received from the Labor Party and within my own party'. But that poor treatment was only going to get worse. Literally minutes after I'd released the statement, the reprisals and retribution began, and they were unbelievable. They were trying everything to introduce silence and fear – to break me.

A well-meaning senior minister called me and said I'd need to 'find myself a good lawyer'. But I *was* a lawyer – and I knew I'd done nothing wrong. Why did I need a lawyer for the defence? Because the prosecution, the party I still belonged to, was making it all up.

From August 2018, I found myself suddenly being diminished in pervasive ways by a stereotypical sexist narrative: a narrative that I was everything from emotionally weak and precious to an aggressive, attention-seeking bully bitch. Because I was loyal to Turnbull, it was reported by the Murdoch media that I was 'Turnbull's puppet' acting for 'revenge' under the guidance of his 'invisible hand'. I was called 'Turnbull's whore' on social media and in vile anonymous correspondence. Emissaries who were obviously seen as close to me were sent to me to seemingly 'just talk'.

But really, their objective was to make me stop talking. Morrison was like a constant menacing background wallpaper, imperceptibly controlling his obliging intermediaries to do his work for him.

Subsequently I found out from various reliable sources that during the agreed twenty-four hours before I released my statement there was intense 'backgrounding' from the PMO and other 'senior Liberal sources' to the media that I was a weak, overemotional woman who had not coped with the coup week. Party leaders added to this narrative in radio and TV interviews within hours of my releasing my media statement.

And then I saw Morrison declaring to a news conference in Sydney, 'What is important right now is *Julia's* welfare ... My first concern is for her welfare and wellbeing ... What am I doing right now? I'm supporting *Julia* and reaching out to *Julia* and giving her every comfort and support for what has been a pretty torrid ordeal for her.'

He kept just using my first name. Like we were somehow close friends or colleagues, which we weren't. As if he was ringing me personally always to 'check in', which he wasn't. It was infuriatingly condescending and misleading.

I felt confused and angry. It was the ultimate PR deflection, at my cost. It's a template he has used again and again to address what, in his mind, is the 'woman's problem' in the context of a 'political situation'.

Even after I announced I would not be recontesting my seat, I tried to continue living my values. I wanted to use whatever time I had left on this esteemed broad public platform to speak honestly, freely and with purpose about matters that people cared about. Climate change action, humanitarian issues – and gender equality. During that period, I made two other speeches that generated publicity: one that night of the Midwinter Ball, to a near-empty chamber, about the need for independent investigatory systems in parliament for workplace misconduct and the urgent imperative for the government to adopt quotas to balance the number of women in parliament, and the other about the plight of the refugees. The louder my voice got, the more attempts were made to stop me.

My speech about refugees was made on 25 October 2018, after a week of my personal consultation and time spent with MPs from across the political divide, important critical stakeholders and the minister responsible. It decried the ramping up of the political football between the parties about the indefinite detention of refugees. I referred to the advocacy of thousands of doctors, the Australian Medical Association and the United Nations High Commissioner for Refugees, and stated it was our 'humanitarian obligation to get these children and their families off Nauru'.

I made the speech in the (again near-empty) House of Representatives chamber at 4:55 pm. At 5.03 pm, Morrison sent me a text message. I'd barely got back to my office. 'Re Nauru, Always happy to take meetings with colleagues on these issues. Always a surprise when they are raised publicly, before being raised privately. Cheers Scott.' (Reprimand.)

By the time I got home from Canberra that night, my phone was melting, including a text from a senior female minister: 'Scomo sent me a text asking if I could advise how to best manage you.' (Control.)

A few days later, Morrison followed up his messages with a 'public bollocking' (as I described it to a friend) in the party room. (Demean.) The sycophantic nodding heads of his new followers were coupled with glaring, hateful stares at me. *So much for the party of free speech*, I thought.

Without any sense of hypocrisy, they continued to try to improve the optics of what was going on by trying to persuade me to act as a 'female prop' – from persistently requesting I ask the 'Dorothy Dixers' in Question Time (the questions planted from within the party to give our politicians the chance to give impressive prepared answers), to requests that I represent Morrison both within and outside my electorate, despite my having made it very clear that I would be doing none of that.

That rainy, scary night, on the drive home from the football, the call that distressed me had been from Morrison. I'm told he made that phone call after flying into Melbourne to attend the very football game I'd missed out on seeing as a special event with my family. I'd been trying to speak to him directly all day – I wanted to tell him directly to get his bully boys to back off. I answered the call and said something along those lines.

In response, he made offers that had been made before by his emissaries including his deputy, who said this would 'take you away from all of this'. He offered to send me to New York as the UN delegate, all expenses paid, for months in a lavish hotel (at taxpayers' cost). I declined. He offered to 'negotiate with Bill [Shorten, then opposition leader] for a pair'. A parliamentary pair is when the two political parties rebalance their numbers for voting when an MP is absent from the chamber for personal, parental or sick leave reasons. It could have effectively meant I'd be on 'unlimited sick leave' or more likely 'unlimited mental health leave' for the remainder of the term. The fact that this would align to the 'emotionally and mentally unwell' narrative was not lost on me. 'I am not sick,' I said.

I believed both offers were made with the sole aim of taking me out of the parliament. Even out of the country. Taking away my voice. Victorian forces wanted (as one Liberal said in a text message) to put me 'under so much pressure that I leave'. I was told they didn't care this would trigger a by-election as they were more concerned I would use parliamentary privilege to 'out them' and their behaviour. Morrison wanted me out too, but needed my vote. This merger of the two forces formed one brutal force. They had different objectives, but they wanted the same outcome. They wanted me silenced.

That night, another feeling of unstoppable determination and resoluteness took a firm hold in me. I wasn't going anywhere on their terms. I wasn't going to limp out of Parliament House with a benign valedictory speech feigning my unfettered loyalty to the party and its leaders. If I were to exit the parliament, I wanted to exit on my terms.

This force planted the seed of something I hadn't previously contemplated: that I could free myself and see out the rest of my term as an independent.

I would have resigned earlier from the party, but I was conscious of a pending state election, and I knew that if I announced 'the jump' before then and they lost, I'd be blamed for the loss, and the backlash would have been even more toxic and cruel. (As it turned out they lost anyway, in a landslide, and many of them blamed me anyway.)

On 27 November 2018, I stood in the chamber of the House of Representatives and announced my decision in what became known as my resignation speech. At one point I said, 'Often when good women call out or are subjected to bad behaviour, the reprisals, backlash and commentary portrays them as the bad ones: the liar, the troublemaker, the emotionally unstable or weak, or someone who should be silenced.'

I'm told it was the first time in history that a speech by a backbench MP was on the front page of every major daily newspaper in the country. I knew that my statements would create a reaction of sorts – I'd seen what had happened in the wake of my social media statement. Confidants, close friends, my loved ones, seasoned politicians whom I'd confided in had warned me. People said things like, 'You'll have to be strong,' 'They'll destroy you,' 'They'll emotionally smash you,' 'Just go quietly for your own sake.' One MP even warned that they would 'kill' me, although I'm sure they didn't mean that in the literal sense. I didn't feel like I was leaving a political party or an employer. I felt like I was leaving a cult.

But I also heard, 'Good on you for speaking your truth,' 'I bloody admire you,' and from one of the most senior female MPs, 'It's the most courageous thing I've ever seen anyone do in this place.'

After I made the speech, I did a focused power walk back to my office, accompanied by my senior staffer, and locked the door. My staff and I couldn't hear each other speak over the phones ringing and someone furiously banging on my office door. I remember thinking, *Geez, that's a determined journalist.* In fact, it was Morrison's deputy. He made it very clear that Morrison wanted me to visit his office. 'He. Is. The. Prime. Minister.' Again, like I'd missed the news cycle. 'You have to go and see him.'

While speaking, the deputy leader was frantically messaging. And I suddenly realised he was messaging whatever I was saying, because as I glanced up to my television, it was all being repeated almost word for word by David Speers on Sky News. In real time.

At one stage I had one minister on the phone who had Morrison in their office, and his deputy in my office (still live-briefing the media), both telling me that he wanted to talk to me, in his office. Morrison clearly preferred that I be the one who was photographed by the throng of media photographers who were now camped outside his office. I said, 'I'm not going to the headmaster's office. He's got my mobile. How about he rings?'

He finally did, several hours later, after that day's Question Time.

Although the core of my resignation speech was referring to the gendered treatment I'd received under his reign and calling for better respect and equality for women, it seemed that the part he was most sensitive about was whether I was going to expose his invisible role as a ringleader – of the coup, and of the treatment I'd received since. He asked the same question in various different ways, along the lines of 'It's not anything I have done is it?' 'You don't have a problem with me, do you?' 'Are you sure there's nothing I've done to make you want to leave?' Would I expose that he was a bully? That he was a man who could not be trusted?

After becoming an independent, I attended a meeting with Morrison and one of my fellow female independent colleagues to discuss the new staffing arrangements and the proposed medevac legislation. It was to be the first – and the last – time I'd meet with him face to face as the prime minister, and my first time in the prime minister's office since the coup. As soon as I walked into the reception area, I sensed what a difference a different leader can make, not just to the position of the office, but to the ambience of the office, the culture and behaviour of the staff. I was greeted tersely, arrogantly, almost dismissively by Morrison's staffer, who promptly disappeared. I glanced around the waiting area, then I literally gasped out loud as my gaze landed on something new, which had replaced the beautiful Indigenous and modern Australian art that had been there in Turnbull's period.

A huge portrait of Queen Elizabeth.

It was eerily metaphorical. Out with the new, in with the old.

As the Queen stared back at me from her portrait I thought,

Well, at least she's a woman. But no chance of Australia becoming a republic under this government.

My fellow crossbench MP colleague arrived and we went into Morrison's office. He seated himself at the head of the table, and his compliant staffer barely lifted his head and not once made eye contact. Morrison leaned back in his chair, put his hands behind his head and manspread as he mansplained why he felt my colleague and I were 'wrong on refugees'.

The meeting at least validated my decision: that there was no place for me in this team, or under this leadership. Some months later Morrison publicly said, 'We want to see women rise. But we don't want to see women rise only on the basis of others doing worse.' I have no doubt he meant it.

*

Many people have asked me whether, knowing what I know now about what I would undergo for leaving the major party in such circumstances, I would do it again. The answer is simple. Yes, I would. I was in a personal position where I could be totally honest and I wasn't concerned with any potential consequences for my future job prospects inside or outside of politics.

But I was not completely fearless then, and I'm not to this day. I did fear what the haters would do. And they did what I feared and then some.

Once I decided to see through my term as an independent, the decision gave me a new energy, fuelled by an enormous team of supporters from across Australia: the general public, the people who came forward to work for me, those who joined my current team of supporters, and those with me on the crossbench. Although the backlash, the whispering campaigns and the abuse continued relentlessly, it didn't stop me from being able to work alongside other independents with trust and mutual respect, and to take the opportunity to give the power of my voice to others. Sitting on the independent crossbench was like being a tennis umpire, with your head going from one side to another, watching the two major parties in a never-ending game – a never-ending power play. But my faith was restored in the fact that, when there is trust and respect, within a team, it drives you to work for the greater good.

During this period, the medevac legislation came through, which made a huge difference to many people's lives. I was able to freely advocate for climate change action and an integrity commission, for truth in political advertising, and of course for an independent reporting system for workplace misconduct and a focus on gender equality.

This transformed experience of politics that I had in my months as an independent suddenly presented me with a different possibility. It informed my brainstorming over the summer as to whether, rather than not recontesting my seat as I had said was my plan while I was still in the Liberal Party, I should go for it and run as an independent in the forthcoming election.

It remains my view that the Liberal Party has reached the 'point of no return' to their self-described 'broad church'. The moderate voice has been drowned out and the party is firmly a Christian, conservative, right-wing party. My vision is that a minority government with moderate, progressive, centre independents holding the balance of power will be the only circuit breaker to the paralysis and political football the major parties have created. Only this will allow real action on matters, such as climate change and gender equality, and allow our country to thrive.

It is an exciting and hopeful vision, but at the time I continued to hesitate about running. One of my closest confidantes and dearest friends said, 'What's stopping you?'

'Fear,' I said. 'They'll really go for me'.

'But Jules, you're like good Sandy from *Grease*. There's no dirt on you.'

'They'll make it up,' I said. I knew them.

Finally, I made the call. I put the residual fear to the back of my mind and rationalised that most of the angst and stress I'd endured was caused when I was within the party, not during my term as an independent. So, in January 2019, I announced my decision to run in the election.

Months earlier, at the time when I announced that I *wasn't* recontesting the election, my husband and I had decided that we would partly relocate and start spending more of our day-to-day lives in our second home on the Mornington Peninsula. It felt like time for a fresh start. This meant that when I subsequently decided to run, I was now running in a different electorate to the one I had won on behalf of the Liberal Party – from the electorate of Chisholm to the electorate of Flinders. The support of the people in my electorate ('Chisholm's loss is Flinders' gain,' they said at farewell events) and of the local community in Flinders was heartwarming.

Not surprisingly, as soon as I made the announcement, the powers that be ramped up their attacks. Together with my new team, we had to brace ourselves for their 'dirty tricks'. I have always made a rule of expecting the unexpected – and in this campaign, there was plenty of that. The Liberal Party were not only running their federal campaign; they were running a vile campaign of bullying and intimidation led and incited by their Machiavellian leaders, who were careful not to show blood on their hands. It was so much worse than anything I experienced from the opposition when I ran in the 2016 campaign.

They continued to use their favourite journalists to voice the frankly absurd concept I was running in the Flinders electorate for 'revenge' on behalf of Turnbull against the current Liberal incumbent, who had served as Peter Dutton's 'wingman' in the leadership coup. We had to be diligent in filtering out 'plants' that had been put all over the electorate, and the more pernicious undercover 'volunteers' who would give a five-dollar donation online and then get access to our campaign material. Party members turned up in 'coincidentally' synchronised timing when the incumbent appeared at prepoll, loudly praising him and then hurling abuse at me. Many unashamedly posted derogatory and defamatory comments on social media. Their activist arm created and letter-boxed weaponised brochures with false and defamatory allegations that aligned to what party members were saying and backgrounding to the press about me. These brochures were distributed the weekend before the election. I took legal action, demanding they cease and desist and destroy the brochures, which they did – but the damage was done. This all went way beyond the 'traditional' behaviour of both the major parties destroying or defacing signage with lewd graffiti.

As election day drew nearer and apparently polls indicated that the race was close, the coordinated attacks seem to intensify and felt like torture. Self-preservation kicked in, and I began to withdraw and decline events and publicity opportunities (including appearing on *Q&A* the Monday before the election). I felt beaten up and spent. I said to my husband in that time, 'If they're doing this because they think I might win, imagine what they'll do if I *do* win.' Part of me was relieved that I didn't win.

Despite all this, running as an independent once again restored my faith in our democratic political system – not just because of the team around me, who were loyal, trustworthy and hardworking, but because the focus was about *people*, not a party.

The road to leadership is made far easier if you believe in the power of people and love building relationships. A big part of doing your job well involves looking after yourself and filling your life with people that you trust. No matter how you might fail, how far you fall, how many accidents or mistakes you make, or how many roadblocks or barriers you face, the leadership journey is a great one if it is surrounded by strong relationships with great people. Rely on your circle of influence whenever going through a challenge – and that challenge can simply be 'not knowing what you're doing' at work. Treasuring and embracing this support will always make you feel strong and courageous.

Far and away, the worst time during my political career, and indeed during my entire career, was that three-month period when I was still a member of the party under Morrison's leadership. I felt the full force of his bullying and political thuggery, supported by the MPs in his 'team', his followers and his friends in the media, and it was underpinned by a particular misogynistic attitude reserved for women leaders.

In October 2020, news reports and social media were filled with snippets of him responding to a story that Christine Holgate, former CEO of Australia Post, had awarded four watches to members of her team for work above and beyond the call of duty – in full compliance with policy. Morrison's voice boomed and his lip curled as he pummelled Christine Holgate's professional reputation, cowardly under the protection of parliamentary privilege, and enunciated the words: 'She. Can. Go.'

I could barely watch repeats of this performance; the flashbacks made me feel sick. Indeed, Christine Holgate confirmed she had medical advice not to watch it, but was shown a recording of it for an interview on ABC's *7.30*. 'I think it is one of the worst acts of bullying I've ever witnessed,' she said in response.

The day of my resignation speech, a cartoon appeared in an article headed 'The Liberals' Woman Problem. Newsflash: it's not women who are the problem'. The cartoon by Matt Golding was a parody of an artwork by the graffiti artist Banksy entitled 'Girl with Balloon', in which a girl stands reaching out to a red balloon that is floating away from her. In the Golding illustration, Morrison's face is depicted in the red balloon and the 'girl' raising her hand is giving the balloon the birdy.

Chapter 10

Looking in the mirror

'If he [Tony Abbott] wants to know what misogyny looks like in modern Australia, he doesn't need a motion in the House of Representatives, he needs a mirror. That's what he needs.' These are the words delivered by our former Prime Minister Julia Gillard to the House in her famous 'misogyny speech'.

Gillard had encountered sexism and misogyny during her term in parliament. At the time she said that gave her the 'emotional start to the speech' and then 'it took on a life of its own'.

I think one of the most powerful elements in the speech is when she says 'he needs a mirror'. A mirror doesn't lie – it shows you what you really look like. When you look into a mirror, though, you should also see the person you feel you are. When the reflection of yourself is looking back at you, you would hope to see a face that stands for the values you hold.

For centuries men and women, but particularly women, in the workforce have been counselled, advised or raised to behave in a way that is not reflective of themselves. To demonstrate a behaviour that isn't reflective of their own values. To not feel or be themselves on the outside.

This advice or counselling is particularly ubiquitous for women who work outside the home and is so normalised that it's barely noticeable. It can come from everywhere, in books, corporate development and mentoring programs, and from friends, sponsors and mentors.

How many of us, particularly women, have been advised to stop using the words 'sorry' or 'just' – or any form of contrition or 'flowery language', for that matter – in our business and working life dialogue? We are instructed to not use flowery language or syntax and to get to the point. And how many of us have taken on the advice? Guilty as charged.

> Version 1: Hi Sally, Thanks so much for our discussion yesterday. Just wondering if you've had a chance to follow up on that matter so you can provide me with the update? Sorry to hassle, I know you're really under the pump but it's better for all of us if we file the update sooner rather than later.

> Version 2: Following up on that matter we discussed yesterday. I need it ASAP.

I studiously took on that advice. After drafts and redrafts of a simple email, I would finally manage to send something along the lines of version 2.

But then I stopped bothering. It took longer to write an email that didn't sound like the way I would talk to the person. My edited 'not sorry' versions felt terse, abrupt, not aligned to my sense of myself or my leadership style – whether or not they were interpreted that way is another thing. I made the judgement call that everyone was better off if I was my authentic self. (I have to add that I'm also as guilty of sending the terse text or email, particularly in a period of time constraints and stress – but I prefer it and feel more myself when I don't.)

It's a prevailing school of thought and advice that women have to take 'sorry 'out of our dialogue – or at least only use it as much as men do. A 2010 study shows that women say 'sorry' more than men do because they have 'a lower threshold for what constitutes offensive behaviour'. But in fact, a person with a higher threshold for what constitutes offensive behaviour is not a good person, let alone a good leader.

I believe 'sorry' is a word that isn't used enough in leadership. It's the best and strongest way to take responsibility for actions and to acknowledge accountability. It can be used to right a wrong.

The fact is, no leader is perfect. Everyone makes mistakes. And perhaps if more men said 'sorry', rather than fewer women, the workplace would be healthier all round. In the workplace misconduct cases that hit the media and drag on in the courts, we often hear the victim say 'all I wanted was an apology'. It's no replacement for tangible action, but 'sorry' clears the air, helps build relationships, recalibrates, puts things right, makes a new start.

Not surprisingly, the opposite – the 'faux' apology, or no apology, or the conditional 'if I've caused offence' apology regularly used by politicians – create the opposite outcome. Cynicism, bitterness, division.

'I'm really sorry it hasn't worked out.' This was the beginning of a tough conversation I had with someone who didn't meet the job requirements during his probationary period. It all went smoothly and respectfully and, some months later, the guy followed up with up with an email thanking me for my honesty, which had ultimately led him to a better career path. Nonetheless, the HR guy also present at the meeting advised me that I was 'too maternal' in my management style and that I shouldn't have said 'sorry'. When I pressed him on what that meant, he said, 'You care too much.' If 'caring too much' about others is a flaw in my leadership style, I'll take it.

I don't believe effective leadership traits are gendered, but I do believe that leadership traits may be demonstrated and weighted differently by male and female leaders. Women's skills in communication and showing empathy are often seen as 'soft skills' rather than essential skills. Gail Kelly, who is ranked among the top ten businesswomen in the world by *Forbes* magazine, after an extraordinary career that included being the first female CEO of one of Australia's big four banks, tells how she 'bristled' when she read commentary from analysts and fund managers along the lines of 'granted she is good with the "soft" stuff of people and culture but it's just as well she has strong bankers around her to handle the financial aspects.'

In modern-day leadership, these skills aren't soft. Rather, it's an imperative to value and build these skills inside organisations across any sector.

In line with the 'don't say sorry' genre, is the 'be more confident and more assertive' mantra. It's an oft-cited argument that one of the main reasons for the gender pay gap is because women aren't assertive enough to ask for a pay rise. This simply isn't true. Research shows that women ask for pay rises as much as men do. The problem is, they don't get them as much as men do.

Hypothetically, if all women did emulate male leaders in the boardrooms, meeting rooms and corridors of power by being more assertive and more confident, not much would get done. How about if we turned this theory on its head and asked some male leaders to be less assertive and not overconfident. Perhaps then there would be less 'manterruptions' and less talking over the few women that are there. Perhaps the diversity of thought and ideas would be able to flourish.

There is nothing like a crisis to create visibility and separate the good and great leaders from the not so good, or to enable people to sniff out a lack of authenticity in a leader: standing behind podiums spurting out meaningless, grandiose message points or doing photo-op poses at the scene, as opposed to making the tough calls, taking real action and rolling their sleeves up to constructively help others, shoulder to shoulder.

During the COVID-19 pandemic we have seen wonderful examples of strong, empathetic and courageous leadership in the corporate sector, from small organisations to large companies. Businesses and divisions have come through the crisis under leaders who share their own vulnerabilities and issues with their teams and are deeply empathetic with their team members' concerns. In many ways, the pandemic has imposed on leaders an obligation to reframe what they might consider to be the most important and effective leadership traits.

There is some research to suggest that female-led countries have fared better under COVID-19. In New Zealand, Prime Minister Jacinda Ardern has been hailed as one of the most effective global leaders in the crisis. I don't believe it's a coincidence that she has stated, and believes, 'I'm very proudly an empathetic, compassionately driven politician. I am trying to chart a different path, and that will attract critics, but I can only be true to myself and the form of leadership I believe in.' She has also said, 'You can be strong, and you can be kind.'

A crisis also reveals gaps in business or policy processes. Gaps that need to be addressed with strong and courageous decision-making, good communication, and compassion and empathy for those affected. Having experienced firsthand the pressure cooker of crisis management during my corporate career, you soon learn that, in high-pressure, high-intensity environments, decisions have to be made quickly and effectively, and it's important to take accountability if mistakes are made and then move forward. Decisions also often need to be made with a balanced mix of courage, compassion and empathy. All these leadership qualities are developed in people based on their lived experiences – and that is why there needs to be a mix of lived experiences at those leadership tables, so that we can get a good mix of qualities in any leadership team.

But it's somehow all and only about women's self-improvement. Somehow, it's women's fault.

For too long women have been told that the reason there's not enough women in leadership is that there are not enough women 'of merit'. To have real merit – and to *show* they have merit – women have to fix their so called 'deficiencies' or work harder. To speak up, speak loudly, ask for the pay rise, be more assertive, wear this, don't wear that, be more assertive, be more confident, to not have so much on their plate and to find balance. To emulate male leaders. To lean in.

No. Just no. There are two major things that get in the way of the merit-based argument: bias (unconscious or otherwise) and discrimination.

In a leadership journey, there are negative power plays everywhere – yes, in different measures at different times, but they're still there. They exist everywhere. The positive power plays, including your own, are characterised by authenticity and the power within yourself. Because the best thing any leader can be is true to themselves and their own leadership style.

*

Brené Brown says: 'There are people who practice being authentic, there are people who don't, and there are the rest of us who are authentic on some days and not so authentic on other days.' Trying to be someone you're not is really hard. And yet 'staying real' and being yourself can often be harder and can take a lot of courage. Particularly in the workplace and in leadership.

Being an authentic leader doesn't mean you always say what you're thinking, in an unfettered way. Authenticity in the workplace and in leadership is full of complexity. These qualities cannot be 'performed'. They have to be real.

I once worked with someone who had been in very senior executive leadership roles all around the world and was on assignment in Australia. For the most part, people loved working with him. He had gravitas, charisma, and importantly he had turned the business around to a more profitable concern and lifted morale. People loved his sense of humour, his honesty, his authenticity – and his humorous way of often using the F-word during executive leadership team meetings. Once, during a meeting with a slightly larger group than the executive team, he dropped the F-word several times – I'm sure myself and the other executive team members didn't even notice. But he picked up something, based on the non-verbal cues of some of the other team members.

The next morning, he asked me one on one, 'Tell me, is using the F-word okay in business meetings in Australia?'

'I think so …' I paused to think about my reaction to it. 'But maybe some people have an issue with it. It's all about context.'

'Yeah, that's what I thought. I sensed they did in that meeting yesterday when I dropped it. A couple of people seemed uncomfortable. I honestly never thought that would be the case in Australia.

I've used the F-word in our exec leadership meetings before ... no more. Okay. No more. Thanks for the lesson. Note to self.'

This may seem like a small thing but, like anything in leadership, from small things big things can grow. He still remained his authentic self, a great sense of humour, a motivational and inspiring leader – but, crucially, he also had good judgement and a willingness to always keep learning.

The best leaders become this way not by doing some empathy or authenticity training course, but by being themselves, having a healthy curiosity, asking questions and adopting an attitude that they don't have all the answers all the time. Noticing that something isn't working and changing it doesn't detract from your authenticity – rather, it enhances it.

Authentic leadership means balancing being honest with people with not making them feel uncomfortable. To be a good leader, you must have both the strength to be the dissenting voice occasionally and the humility to accept that your opinion, while strongly held, may not be the one that's going to fly. You must advocate for change, but also have the strength to cope with backlash. You must learn how to say what's on your mind but without offending people.

Being authentic means setting your own boundaries and having the courage to recognise that you, and everyone else who's taken that journey, including those before you and after you, are not perfect. It means believing you are 'enough' to get there and being grateful for that.

Being true to yourself certainly doesn't mean you shouldn't be open to constructive criticism. Openness to feedback is a highly valuable and often underrated leadership tool, as is a willingness to always keep learning.

Luckily, in my corporate career, I've worked with organisations that always put a value on performance reviews. I've sat through countless of my own, and those of people I've managed and lead, as well as participated in numerous executive leadership team reviews of the emerging or potential leaders.

In one-on-one reviews, the review can start like this: 'You've met all the key deliverables, you've gone above and beyond the call of duty, you show great leadership skills, you have massive potential – but ...' Many people listen to all the great feedback, usually delivered first, but don't *really* listen to it – they're waiting for the 'but', on the assumption that the 'but' is going to be something negative. Instead of appreciating the praise and considering the value of the constructive criticism, they skip straight to getting defensive, or think it's rubbish and ignore it. In the process, they are passing up an opportunity to learn and grow as a leader or potential leader.

Of course, you also don't need to take on all feedback to be a good leader, especially when that 'feedback' advises you in some form or other to be someone that you're not. Like once, when someone more senior than me told me upon my promotion that I should maintain an air of mystique around anything going on in my personal life: 'Keep a work face and a home face.' That wasn't me. I believe people need to see all the real faces of their leaders.

It's important to recognise, distil and accept constructive feedback from people you respect. And to learn to recognise the feedback that's a thinly disguised rehashing of the stereotypes – too old, too young, too weak, too strong, too difficult. Your doubts and analysis as to whether feedback is constructive or not, whether it's based on bias, unconscious bias, or not well-founded for any reason, is best helped by airing your thoughts and talking it out with one or more trusted friends, work colleagues or loved ones. People who know more about you as a whole person.

It's also good to take this approach when it comes to our biggest critics: our inner critics. And remind yourself that 'perfection is the enemy of good'.

'I've worked all around the world with lawyers more senior than you, on major transactions, deals litigation, crisis and risk management – and the very best thing about you is your sense of humour.' That feedback, which I've always cherished, came from a CEO with whom I worked for many years. The value of humour (the caveat being, not inappropriate humour) and being able to laugh not only with those you love but simply with those with whom you work is integral to life and so often overlooked. By incorporating a sense of humour into your working life, you can forge stronger connections with your team, let in lessons that might be harder to digest without a laugh, and find a way to cope with those moments when your outcomes might be further from perfect than usual.

The most agile and successful companies are those that embrace authentic leaders as much as the leaders embrace the values of the company. By far and away the best organisations to work for, and I've been lucky enough to work for several of them, are those whose values are aligned to your own. And not just the values as they are listed on a PowerPoint slide.

Perfection in most of our working lives remains enduringly aspirational, and there will be good times and bad. There may well be leaders, line managers, partners, senior associates or others who are your seniors where you'll find your values are completed misaligned with theirs. Of course, there are times where you will have a differing view to the majority and where you will have to 'go with' the company position, or the majority decision, or what 'the boss' says.

But there may be times when you believe the only option to be true to yourself is to plan a way out.

When I left the Liberal Party, many tried to persuade me to change my mind. They could see that my seat was a big risk. One MP even called and added to his unsophisticated art of persuasion skills by saying, 'This women thing – don't you think it would be better to try and fix it from the inside?'

Unlike so many MPs, I'd worked on the 'outside' for many more years than I worked on the inside, and some made the absurd assumption that that was why I wasn't cut out for it. I responded in my resignation speech: 'To those who say politics is not for the faint hearted and that women have to "toughen up", I say this: the hallmark characteristics of the Australian woman – and I've met thousands of them, be they in my local community, in politics, in business, the media and sport – are resilience and a strong, authentic, independent spirit.'

What underpinned my resolute tone during that speech was that my values had become so misaligned to those of the new leadership. By some serendipitous coincidence, the federal treasurer and newly installed prime minister had scheduled a press conference at exactly the same time as my speech on leaving the Liberal Party. When they received a question about their 'women problem', their marketing-driven answer was more validation that I'd made the right decision, and was given that final flourish with 'the daughter defence':

> TREASURER: Can I just add to that. I'm a proud dad of a young daughter and Scott, the Prime Minister, is a proud dad of two young daughters. We want our party to provide the best opportunity for our daughters.

PRIME MINISTER: That's right.

TREASURER: And it is. So, we are part of a party that believes in their aspiration and their hope. So, this view that some in the media are trying to promote, is wrong. The reality is our party will deliver the best possible outcomes for my daughters and Scott's daughters.

In March 2020, the very impressive US congresswoman Alexandria Ocasio-Cortez called out the behaviour of a Republican congressman, who had called her a 'f---ing bitch'. The speech will remain as one of the most powerful speeches about misogyny, next to our own Julia Gillard's misogyny speech. In the context of what purported to be an apology, the congressman said, 'Having been married for forty-five years with two daughters, I'm very cognisant of my language.' And in AOC's powerful reply she said, 'What I do have issue with is using women, our wives and daughters as shields and excuses for poor behaviour.'

All women are someone's daughters. To provide an answer to any type of 'women problem' by saying you have a daughter just reinforces that there's a problem. The women's problem is not just a problem for women. It's a problem for men and women. Men in power who have daughters aren't automatically entitled to some fictional 'daughter defence'.

Morrison has told us that he loves his wife, daughters and mother, as if it is some kind of novelty. It is not surprising that he used the daughter defence again after the criticism of his initial response to the harrowing story of Brittany Higgins. Morrison had consulted his wife, Jenny, whom he praised with having 'a way of clarifying things', and she had told him to consider what had happened to Higgins 'as a father' of daughters. Teagan George, a reporter for Channel 10 news, responded with the question, 'Shouldn't you have thought about it as a human being? What happens if men don't have a wife and children, would they reach the same compassionate conclusion?' In her National Press Club address, Grace Tame powerfully spoke out against Morrison's use of the phrase 'as a father': 'it shouldn't take having children to have a conscience. And actually on top of that, having children doesn't guarantee a conscience.'

After my resignation speech, my inbox and phone lines were both swamped – with a roughly even number of messages of hate and of support. The death threats and abuse were counterbalanced by the messages of support from people of all walks of life – from across Australia and internationally. And particularly from women.

This included hundreds of people of all ages with their stories of having been victims of harassment, assault, bullying and general workplace misconduct. A number of women had left their careers and been silenced by virtue of a non-disclosure agreement, or they were still suffering and enduring because they didn't feel safe to report these instances and it would threaten their livelihood. The common theme was that these issues were never resolved for them: they were either too frightened to challenge powerful forces or they'd done so unsuccessfully and been compelled to leave that workplace – and in many situations leave their careers.

I hoped my honesty would bring about some change for the future. I hoped it would inspire women to use their own personal power – that which is on the inside. Power you have to dig deep for, and which resides embedded in your values, your principles. It's a power that doesn't have to have the title to go with it.

Leaders who are able to identify and address gaps during a crisis. Leaders who are openly active about social issues and equality. Leaders who are willing to accept that previous processes or structures may not be working and need review or change – be that to address structural sexism or other forms of bias, barriers or discrimination. Leaders who share our values. These are the leaders we should all aspire to be. These are the sorts of leaders that we should all expect to work for. But it doesn't always work out that way.

No matter the sector, no matter if you're a member of the team or the team leader, if your view on the 'inside' of your workplace culture is that there's no alignment of your personal values to those in leadership and that you cannot be your authentic self, then it's best to get out. Sometimes you just can't change things from the inside. Being a leader doesn't just mean being the boss. It means working for and with the people around you, with purpose, and if you're not able to do that, then your leadership is not worth much. Instead, once you're out, use your personal power – for your own good and for the good of others. You don't need positional power to advocate or influence to make changes, whether they are large or small.

*

When I announced that I was to be an independent MP, author Nikki Gemmell said, 'The eloquent, audacious, courageous statement of disruption from @JuliaBanksMP goes to the nub of why voters are disaffected with our major parties. Haters will go for her – I wish her courage for the months ahead. She'll go down in history for calling out truth to power.'

Others asked me how it felt to be so powerful, the one who had left the government struggling to keep control of the House of Representatives as 'the majority of one' went to the crossbench. A fellow MP asked the question, 'How's it feel to be the most powerful person in the country right now?'

Powerful is certainly not how I felt at that time. I was still under siege and had acquired a whole new set of opponents who were fiercer than ever. I would often look back and read Gemmell's quote, to give me a personal and emotional boost that helped me fend off the 'haters'. But by serving and running as an independent, trust in people in and around the body politic had re-entered my life. And for that reason, I felt my personal power returning.

During that period, I was in the make-up rooms of the ABC studios, about to do my first ever appearance on *Q&A*. One of my fellow independent MPs was sitting next to me and, probably trying to stave off our respective nerves, we were making general chitchat and musing about what a luxury it was to get our make-up done professionally. I felt exhausted and said to the make-up artist that I needed heavy duty make-up, because I probably looked like I'd aged dramatically given what I'd been through those last few months.

'Are you kidding?' said my colleague and friend. 'Everyone is saying how you look at least ten years younger since you announced you're an independent. I mean it. Look in the mirror!'

'Nooo,' I protested.

'Seriously, look in the mirror'

As I looked in the mirror, I knew what was different. The image looking back at me was the real me on the inside. Regardless of whether I had heavy duty make-up applied or whether I actually looked younger, that sense of personal power I was feeling really reflected back to me in that mirror image.

During the immediate aftermath of my unsuccessful bid to be elected as an independent, my sense of personal power felt beaten down. I experienced a number of symptoms that aligned with post-traumatic stress. One day during that period, I was travelling on a tram into the city, listening to a podcast on my airpods, when a well-dressed businessman tapped me on the shoulder.

'Excuse me, are you Julia Banks?'

'Yes,' I said, immediately bracing myself for the negativity I'd grown so accustomed to.

'I just want you to know, you're an inspiration to my children – my sons and daughters. We all think you're amazing for what you did. Please keep going.'

That moment made me feel powerful.

I didn't feel powerful because I was on the front page of every newspaper or in the media every other day, or because I had been an MP or a corporate business leader. Or because I had 'spoken truth to power'.

I felt powerful because I was true to myself – by just being myself. And I felt powerful because I had embraced and valued the power of people in my life and work. I felt powerful because I knew I'd made a difference to others, be they the individuals in communities I've advocated for, the people on the teams I'd led, or any of the other people I'd worked with. These moments, the very best feelings of power, come when courage, passion and purpose, and staying true to your values, all collide at once.

In anyone's individual leadership journey, bias and barriers may look very similar or sometimes be quite different. They may occur at different times, in different settings and involve different people. If you want to overcome them and get to a destination yourself, you might consult with family, friends, work colleagues, leaders, mentors or role models. You might use references, read books, attend conferences, acquire knowledge and tips from networking events, learn from the experiences of others, ask people for advice, even emulate them.

But along the way, at every point, it's you who's making the decisions. If you want to go on that journey, whether in life or work, you don't ask someone else to do it for you. Only you can assess the consequences of any decisions you have made or might make. If you decide to go in a certain direction at a certain time, you're doing that yourself.

The experience might sometimes feel outside your comfort zone. You can be heading into unknown territory, take a wrong turn, need to stop for a break or not be really clear on your destination. You might hit an unexpected barrier or roadblock. But the lessons you will learn and the skills you will develop from having to navigate that discomfort is why lived experience is the best experience of all.

Progress may come when you expect it and not at other times, and of course your drive and sense of ambition will change at different points of your life and career – whether that means making money as opposed to only finding 'meaning' in your work, taking an unexpected opportunity, or deciding to step up into a new leadership role. It's important to pay attention and sometimes decide that you're enough where you are, that you've reached where you want to be, at least for that point in time. That your success is your success and doesn't mean you have to be at the very top branch of the tree.

While everything in leadership can seem like a rush, it is always good to remember the gift of time. I once worked with an astute global leader who had at least twenty years more experience than I did in crisis management. I was briefing him on a matter and explaining that, in retrospect, we would have done a few things differently. He simply said, 'Look, if you want to decide what to do next in a crisis, wait ten minutes.' Similarly, when you are faced with a big choice or a stressful situation at work, take the time to breathe and to consider your options. But it remains important to remember that life moves fast, we're not on this earth for very long, and leadership opportunities often come at an inconvenient time. Sometimes you just have to dive in because your gut tells you it's the right thing to do. Never underestimate trusting your instincts. They rarely let you down.

Your authentic self, your courage and your values are what drives the power in you. Sometimes the outcomes might not be what you anticipated. Sometimes you'll make mistakes or bad judgement calls. It's that power that enables you to come up from failure, to steel yourself with courage and resilience for challenging times, and for the inevitable backlash if you want to change something or do something outside of the norm.

It's the power in you that will enable you to make good decisions – and not just for yourself. The best power plays, the times where you feel you're most powerful, are the times when you use your power to lead for the benefit of others.

SOURCES

INTRODUCTION

'Because it's 2015.' Jessica Murphy, 'Trudeau gives Canada first cabinet with equal number of men and women', *Guardian*, 5 November 2015, theguardian.com/world/2015/nov/04/canada-cabinet-gender-diversity-justin-trudeau

That five-minute speech ... Julia Banks, Australian House of Representatives, House Hansard, 27 November 2018, pp. 11571–72.

CHAPTER 1: That girl will go places

'You can't be what you can't see' Attributed to Marian Wright Edelman, American civil rights activist.

'While I may be the first woman ...' Kamala Harris, victory speech on becoming US vice-president, NBC News, nbcnews.com/video/watch-kamala-harris-full-victory-speech-as-vice-president-elect-95525445787

'hated the very word ...' Anna Fels, 'Do women lack ambition?', *Harvard Business Review*, April 2004, hbr.org/2004/04/do-women-lack-ambition

'Mum's focus on ensuring ...' Julia Banks, Australian House of Representatives, House Hansard, Thursday 18 October, 'Lolatgis, Mrs Helen'.

'We learn early ...' Mona Eltahawy, *The Seven Necessary Sins for Women and Girls*, Beacon Press, 2019, p. 82.

'there's something about her I just don't like' *A Podcast of One's Own with Julia Gillard*, Acast, 16 October 2020, play.acast.com/s/a-podcast-of-ones-own/jenniferpalmierionthe2020uselection

'That's what I do.' Shoshana Walter, '"I'm a non-political person," Mrs. Biden says', The Ledger, 25 October 2008, theledger.com/article/LK/20081025/News/608128388/LL

Dr Julia Baird has borne the wrath ... Julia Baird (@bairdjulia), 12 February 2018, twitter.com/bairdjulia/status/962867967515025408

'embedded ... mechanisms that silence women ...' Mary Beard, *Women & Power: A Manifesto*, Allen & Unwin, 2017, p. xiii.

CHAPTER 2: Dressed for battle

A study conducted by Gender Equity Victoria ... Media, Entertainment & Arts Alliance & Gender Equity Victoria, *Don't Read the Comments: Enhancing Online Safety for Women Working in the Media*, 2019, genvic.org.au/wp-content/uploads/2019/10/GV_MEAA_PolicyDoc_V5_WEB.pdf

'Men are serious, women are silly ...' Helen Lewis, *Difficult Women: A History of Feminism in 11 Fights*, Random House, 2020.

'bloody difficult woman' Laura Kuenssberg, 'What Theresa May's "difficult woman" line reveals', BBC News, 2 May 2017, bbc.com/news/uk-politics-39787355

'If you stand for equality, then you're a feminist – I'm sorry to tell you.' *A HeForShe Conversation with Emma Watson*, 8 March 2015, youtu.be/LNi9Ypc0cg8

'If we're too tough, we're unlikeable ...' Hillary Rodham Clinton, *What Happened*, Simon & Schuster, 2017, p. 119.

CHAPTER 3: Never too young

That evidence doesn't in fact exist. Catherine Fox, *Stop Fixing Women: Why Building Fairer Workplaces Is Everyone's Business*, NewSouth, 2017, p. 62.

power is given to leaders by those in the team ... Dacher Keltner, *This Working Life*, ABC Radio National, 8 February 2021, abc.net.au/radionational/programs/this-working-life/power-at-work/13125588

'Younger workers believed ...' Eden King, Lisa Finkelstein, Courtney Thomas & Abby Corrington, 'Generational differences at work are small. Thinking they're big affects our behavior', *Harvard Business Review*, 1 August 2019, hbr.org/2019/08/generational-differences-at-work-are-small-thinking-theyre-big-affects-our-behavior

'take the earliest exit possible off the fossil fuel highway' Michael Mann, 'For Australia's sake, I hope Trump's climate science denialism loses', *Guardian*, 17 October 2020, theguardian.com/commentisfree/2020/oct/17/for-australias-sake-i-hope-trumps-climate-science-denialism-loses

'children are not just adults-in-waiting ...' Kate Douglas, 'Friday essay: why we need children's life stories like I Am Greta', The Conversation, 23 October 2020, theconversation.com/friday-essay-why-we-need-childrens-life-stories-like-i-am-greta-148178

'Life should be full **of career changes ...'** 'Patrice Newell, age-63, organic farmer / author / climate warrior', The Silver Women, August 2020, thesilverwomen.com/patrice-newell/

CHAPTER 4: Power and prejudice

'a heartfelt plea, asking the Australian parliament ...' Michael Sweet, 'Julia Banks' call from the heart', *Neos Kosmos*, 19 September 2016, neoskosmos.com/en/38234/julia-banks-call-from-the-heart/

'In my first speech ...' Pauline Hanson, Australian Senate, Senate Hansard, 14 September 2016, p. 937.

'hardwired insecurity ... an ingrained sensibility ...' 'ABC Indigenous journalist Miriam Corowa on cultural diversity in TV news and her personal struggles and triumphs', ABC News, 29 August 2020, abc.net.au/news/redirects/backstory/2020-08-29/abc-news-indigenous-journalist-miriam-corowa-media-diversity/12604298

'If you walk into a room with investors ...' Jessica Yun, 'The bamboo ceiling 2021: the "double whammy" Asian women face in their careers', Yahoo Finance, 8 March 2021, au.sports.yahoo.com/bamboo-ceiling-iwd-2021-023047411.html

'This catastrophe now engulfing the polity ...' Phillip Coorey, 'You can blame the poms, not the wogs, for this citizenship crisis', *Australian Financial Review*, 10 November 2017, afr.com/politics/you-can-blame-the-poms-not-the-wogs-for-this-citizenship-crisis-20171110-gzifms

'seriously contending that the House ...' Malcolm Turnbull, Australian House of Representatives, House Hansard, 6 December 2017, p. 12875.

'main legacy', 'bringing to light ...' Nikos Fotakis, 'Julia Banks' shining hour – the MP who brought a sitting PM to Oakleigh', *Neos Kosmos*, 14 February 2019, neoskosmos.com/en/129399/julia-banks-shining-hour/

'Biden and Harris represent an utter repudiation of the Trump era.' Anne Summers, 'Trump's worst nightmare: Kamala Harris is a repudiation of his era', *Sydney Morning Herald*, 15 August 2020, smh.com.au/world/north-america/trump-s-worst-nightmare-kamala-harris-is-a-repudiation-of-his-era-20200813-p55li8.html

'Maori culture is increasingly seen ...' Laura Tingle, 'How a catastrophic global pandemic has given Australia a new lens on New Zealand', ABC News, 28 November 2020, abc.net.au/news/2020-11-28/what-australia-can-learn-from-new-zealand/12922956

'final solution' Fraser Anning, Australian Senate, Senate Hansard, 14 August 2018, p. 4717.

'as they felt the need to justify ...' Phillip Coorey, 'Fraser Anning forces parliament to wake up', *Australian Financial Review*, 15 August 2018, afr.com/politics/fraser-anning-forces-parliament-to-wake-up-20180815-h13zco

my opinion piece in support ... Julia Banks, 'Liberal MP: this is why I'm campaigning for "yes"', *Sydney Morning Herald*, 24 October 2017, smh.com.au/opinion/liberal-mp-this-is-why-im-campaigning-for-yes-20171024-gz6z6k.html; Michael Sweet, 'Why I'm voting "yes": MP Julia Banks opens up on same-sex marriage', *Neos Kosmos*, 27 October 2017, neoskosmos.com/en/44067/mp-julia-banks-same-sex-marriage-why-im-voting-yes/

'We've voted today for equality, for love.' Malcolm Turnbull, Australian House of Representatives, House Hansard, 7 December 2017, p. 13144.

CHAPTER 5: Having your all

'Women can have it all ...' Nick Robins-Early, 'Madeleine Albright: women can have it all, just not at the same time', *New York Magazine*, 29 March 2013, nymag.com/intelligencer/2013/03/madeleine-albright-women-have-it-all.html

'are experiencing a different middle age ...' Ada Calhoun, 'Gen-X women are caught in a generational tug-of-war', *The Atlantic*, 8 January 2020, theatlantic.com/family/archive/2020/01/generation-x-women-are-facing-caregiving-crisis/604510/

there is a traditional model of the woman at home ... Annabel Crabb, *The Wife Drought*, Penguin, 2015, pp. 218–19.

'If she wants children and a job ...' Caitlin Moran, *More Than A Woman*, Penguin, 2020.

'The glass ceiling ...' Julia Banks, Australian House of Representatives, House Hansard, 15 September 2016, p. 1095.

women earn 18 per cent less than men ... Catherine Fox, *Stop Fixing Women: Why Building Fairer Workplaces Is Everyone's Business*, NewSouth, 2017, p. 76.

'working part-time includes a reduction ...' Workplace Gender Equality Agency, *Unpaid Care Work and the Labour Market*, Australian Government, 2016, wgea.gov.au/sites/default/files/documents/australian-unpaid-care-work-and-the-labour-market.pdf

disproportionate amount of unpaid work women do ... Kristine Ziwica, 'Yes pandemic parental burnout is a thing and you're not alone', Women's Agenda, 10 September 2020, womensagenda.com.au/life/jugglehood/yes-pandemic-parental-burnout-is-a-thing-and-youre-not-alone/

'How lucky was I ...' Kate Ellis, *BroadTalk*, Acast, 13 August 2020, play.acast.com/s/broadtalk/kateellis

'I'm not sure that you will ever have a fifty/fifty thing ...' John Howard, address to National Press Club, Canberra, 7 September 2016.

'It is never right to say never ...' Julia Banks, Australian House of Representatives, House Hansard, 15 September 2016, p. 1094.

CHAPTER 6: The only woman in the room

'How Julia Banks made [ANZ CEO] Shayne Elliott squirm' Fleur Anderson, 'How Julia Banks made Shayne Elliott squirm over ANZ's "blokey culture"', *Australian Financial Review*, 5 October 2016, afr.com/politics/how-julia-banks-made-shayne-elliott-squirm-over-anzs-blokey-culture-20161005-grvb1h

'waiting for Julia Banks MP to get to the point of her question' Matt Keough (@mattkeough), 8 March 2017, twitter.com/mattkeogh/status/839311940665016320

there is a 4.9 per cent increase in company ... Rebecca Cassells & Alan Duncan, *Gender Equity Insights 2020: Delivering the Business Outcomes*, Bankwest Curtin Economics Centre & Australian Workplace Gender Equality Agency Gender Equity Series, no. 5, March 2020, bcec.edu.au/assets/2020/06/BCEC-WGEA-Gender-Equity-Insights-2020-Delivering-the-Business-Outcomes.pdf

When President Obama took office ... Juliet Eilperin, 'White House women want to be in the room where it happens', *Washington Post*, 13 September 2016, washingtonpost.com/news/powerpost/wp/2016/09/13/white-house-women-are-now-in-the-room-where-it-happens/

'I'm speaking, Mr Vice President, I'm speaking' Cady Lang, '"Mr. Vice President, I'm speaking." What research says about men interrupting women – and how to stop it', *Time*, 9 October 2020, time.com/5898144/men-interrupting-women/

'Ask yourself as you participate in discussions ...' Julia Gillard & Ngozi Okonjo-Iweala, *Women and Leadership: Real Lives, Real Lessons*, Penguin, 2020, p. 294.

'Inside the Canberra Bubble' *Four Corners*, ABC TV, 9 November 2020, abc.net.au/4corners/inside-the-canberra-bubble/12864676

'human frailty' Scott Morrison, press conference, 10 November 2020, pm.gov.au/media/press-conference-australian-parliament-house-act-29

'there is a special place in hell ...' 'special place of honour' 'Madeleine Albright: my undiplomatic moment', *New York Times*, 12 February 2016, nytimes.com/2016/02/13/opinion/madeleine-albright-my-undiplomatic-moment.html

'If they complained ...' Niki Savva, *Plots and Prayers: Malcolm Turnbull's Demise and Scott Morrison's Ascension*, Scribe Publications, 2019, p. 295.

'Labor solution to a Liberal problem' Rosie Lewis & Richard Ferguson, 'Quotas an option for Liberal Party women', *Australian*, 5 January 2019, theaustralian.com.au/nation/politics/quotas-an-option-for-liberal-party-women/news-story/32ac180be3441c540c26c670d8dab59e.

'attack Banks', 'take on Banks', 'to her great credit' Michael Kroger, 'Morrison was always in front, we just didn't know it', *Sydney Morning Herald*, 21 May 2019, smh.com.au/federal-election-2019/morrison-was-always-in-front-we-just-didn-t-know-it-20190520-p51p96.html

'Not here because of [my] skirt' Richard Ferguson, 'Not here for my skirt, says promoted senator', *Australian*, 27 May 2019, theaustralian.com.au/nation/politics/not-here-for-my-skirt-says-promoted-senator/news-story/9b1d3fada57b00b4243139e326a4a31f.

'mainly women who are involved …' 'Mentoring has largely failed …' Catherine Fox, *Stop Fixing Women: Why Building Fairer Workplaces Is Everyone's Business*, NewSouth, 2017, p. 135, 123.

instead of 'mentors', you should look for 'champions' Cindy Gallop & Tomas Chamorro-Premuzic, '7 pieces of bad career advice women should ignore', *Harvard Business Review,* 15 April 2021, hbr.org/2021/04/7-pieces-of-bad-career-advice-women-should-ignore

'Many companies need to do more …' Jess Huang, Alexis Krivkovich, Irina Starikova, Lareina Yee & Delia Zanoschi, *Women in the Workplace 2019*, McKinsey & Company, 2019, womenintheworkplace.com/2019

1205 people have been elected … Parliamentary Library, Canberra, May 2021.

Australia has dropped to fifty. World Economic Forum, *Global Gender Gap Report 2021*, 2021, weforum.org/docs/WEF_GGGR_2021.pdf

'unpalatable' and 'undemocratic'. Nick Cater & Nicolle Flint, *Gender & Politics 2020: The Path towards Real Diversity*, Menzies Research Centre, 2020, menziesrc.org/report-store/gender-amp-politics-2020-the-path-towards-real-diversity

My speech that night was about quotas. Julia Banks, Australian House of Representatives, House Hansard, 12 September 2018, p. 8860.

'open to the conversation' Scott Morrison, press conference, 23 March 2021, pm.gov.au/media/press-conference-australian-parliament-house-act-37

'lively debate' Annabel Crabb, 'Julia Gillard's portrait unveiled in Parliament House', ABC News, 24 October 2018, abc.net.au/news/2018-10-24/julia-gillard-portrait-unveiled-in-parliament-house/10424304

CHAPTER 7: Never too old

'a British survey does put middle age …' Richard Alleyne, 'Middle age begins at 35 and ends at 58', *The Telegraph*, 16 March 2010, telegraph.co.uk/news/health/news/7458147/Middle-age-begins-at-35-and-ends-at-58.html

'Say "fuck off" more and stop being so bloody polite' Michelle Lee, 'Why Helen Mirren wishes she'd said "fuck off" more as a young woman', Allure, 14 August 2017, allure.com/story/helen-mirren-cover-story-september-2017

most received no employer support … British Medical Association, *Challenging the Culture on Menopause for Working Doctors*, 2020, bma.org.uk/media/2913/bma-challenging-the-culture-on-menopause-for-working-doctors-report-aug-2020.pdf

'When people talk about not being whistled at …' Gaby Hinsliff, '"A weird liberation": why women are exposing the wild truth about midlife and menopause', *Guardian*, 22 September 2020, theguardian.com/lifeandstyle/2020/sep/22/weird-liberation-women-wild-truth-midlife-menopause

Australia's fastest-growing group homeless population … Jane Caro, 'The outlook for older women in Australia is dire – but no one seems to care', *Guardian*, 23 November 2020, theguardian.com/commentisfree/2020/nov/23/the-outlook-for-older-women-in-australia-is-dire-but-no-one-seem-to-care

'"big boys" who had PhDs and masters in economics' Aaron Patrick, 'Female Liberal MPs look like an endangered species', *Australian Financial Review*, 15 March 2017, afr.com/politics/federal/female-liberal-mps-look-like-an-endangered-species-20170307-gus4sq

'Women are born with pain …' Phoebe Waller-Bridge (writer) & Harry Bradbeer (director), *Fleabag*, series 2, episode 3, BBC, 2019.

'Grin Reapers' Anna Caldwell, 'Grin Reapers', *Daily Telegraph* (Sydney), 13 February 2019.

'Labor mutton dressed as Liberal lamb' Peta Credlin, 'Beware the Labor mutton dressed as Liberal lamb', *Daily Telegraph* (Sydney), 2 February 2019.

'You don't own me ...' Julia Banks, statement on deleted Twitter account @juliabanksMP, 22 May 2019; Sarah Martin, 'Julia Banks bows out of politics with parting shot at the "haters"', *Guardian*, 22 May 2019, theguardian.com/australia-news/2019/may/22/julia-banks-bows-out-of-politics-with-parting-shot-at-haters.

'owe a lot' John Howard, *7.30*, ABC TV, 27 November 2018, abc.net.au/7.30/john-howard-on-the-victorian-election,-coalition/10560318

CHAPTER 8: To speak or not to speak

'Why is it the woman's burden ...', 'a complicated one ...' Jodi Kantor & Megan Twohey, *She Said*, Penguin Random House, 2019, p. 2.

since 2010, more people meet their partner online ... Catherine Hanrahan, 'More people now meet their partner online than through friends or work combined', ABC News, 26 November 2019, abc.net.au/news/2019-11-26/australia-talks-national-survey-where-to-find-a-partner/11692170

2020 independent investigation findings ... Kate McClymont & Jacqueline Maley, 'High Court inquiry finds former justice Dyson Heydon sexually harassed associates', *Sydney Morning Herald*, 22 June 2020, smh.com.au/national/high-court-inquiry-finds-former-justice-dyson-heydon-sexually-harassed-associates-20200622-p5550w.html

the new chief executive Boe Pahari was asked ... Michael Roddan, 'AMP must come clean on Pahari, says accuser', *Australian Financial Review*, 17 August 2020, afr.com/companies/financial-services/amp-must-come-clean-on-pahari-says-accuser-20200814-p55lw3

'I would just make sure …' John Fraser, *No Limitations*, episode 41, Blenheim Partners & Spotify, May 2020, open.spotify.com/episode/1j0qus4TsHhKXZBaolM7vu

'There are so very few false allegations …' Julia Baird, 'Dinosaurs thrive when nothing ever changes', *Sydney Morning Herald*, 11 July 2020, smh.com.au/national/dinosaurs-thrive-when-nothing-ever-changes-20200710-p55aw8.html

'We keep men's secrets …' Virginia Trioli, 'Brittany Higgins raised her voice loudly – and she can't be the only one who does', ABC News, 20 February 2021, abc.net.au/news/2021-02-20/brittany-higgins-raised-her-voice-loudly-cant-only-one/13169858

'Inside the Canberra Bubble' *Four Corners*, ABC TV, 9 November 2020, abc.net.au/4corners/inside-the-canberra-bubble/12864676

'It was fascinating in the lead-up to the story …' Amanda Meade, '"Siege mentality" as ABC's Four Corners bursts Canberra bubble', *Guardian*, 13 November 2020, theguardian.com/australia-news/commentisfree/2020/nov/13/siege-mentality-as-abcs-four-corners-bursts-canberra-bubble

'time-honoured "internal review" …' Peter Hartcher, 'Monstrous act exposes the cold inhumanity at the heart of the Morrison government', *Sydney Morning Herald*, 20 February 2021, smh.com.au/politics/federal/monstrous-act-exposes-the-cold-inhumanity-at-the-heart-of-the-morrison-government-20210219-p5745m.html

Morrison's over-familiarity … Jacqueline Maley, 'Call her Ms Higgins: the PM's over-familiarity is revealing', *Sydney Morning Herald*, 21 February 2021, smh.com.au/politics/federal/call-her-ms-higgins-the-pm-s-over-familiarity-is-revealing-20210219-p5743o.html

'The continued victim-blaming rhetoric …' Katharine Murphy, 'Brittany Higgins accuses prime minister of using "victim-blaming rhetoric" after alleged rape', *Guardian*, 17 February 2021, theguardian.

com/australia-news/2021/feb/17/brittany-higgins-accuses-prime-minister-of-using-victim-blaming-rhetoric-after-alleged

'I was sick to my stomach ...' Samantha Maiden, 'Scott Morrison image that made Brittany Higgins speak out about alleged rape', News.com.au, 16 February 2021, news.com.au/national/politics/scott-morrison-image-that-made-brittany-higgins-speak-out-about-alleged-rape/news-story/cd43fee050269e4d3f9dc0f17dfa7b38

'emotional and mental abuse of the very highest order ...' Jenna Price, 'Is the Liberal Party running a protection racket?', *Canberra Times*, 18 February 2021, canberratimes.com.au/story/7133149/is-the-liberal-party-running-a-protection-racket/

'When I was asked to speak here today ...' Julia Banks, speech at March4Justice rally, Treasury Gardens, Melbourne, 15 March 2021.

'a death spiral' Peter Hartcher, 'A death spiral Morrison struggles to arrest', *Sydney Morning Herald*, 27 March 2021, smh.com.au/politics/federal/a-death-spiral-morrison-struggles-to-arrest-20210326-p57ehj.html

'met with bullets' Scott Morrison, Australian House of Representatives, House Hansard, 15 March 2021, p. 62.

'glass houses', 'be careful' Scott Morrison, press conference, 23 March 2021, pm.gov.au/media/press-conference-australian-parliament-house-act-37

swift action taken ... Paul Karp, 'Coalition staffer sacked for alleged sex act on female MP's desk was longtime Liberal aide', *Guardian*, 23 March 2021, theguardian.com/australia-news/2021/mar/23/coalition-staffer-sacked-for-alleged-sex-act-on-female-mps-desk-was-longtime-liberal-aide

'pushing the women's business to the women ...' Jane Caro, *The Drum*, ABC TV, 29 March 2021, abc.net.au/news/2021-03-29/the-drum:-monday-march-29/13280654

'We need to be careful ...' *Kerry O'Brien in Conversation with Grace Tame, Australian of the Year 2021*, Home of the Arts & Griffith University, 30 March 2021, betterfuture.griffith.edu.au/grace-tame-livestream/

'prime minister for women' Scott Morrison, press conference, 29 March 2021, pm.gov.au/media/press-conference-australian-parliament-house-act-38

'control freak' Malcolm Turnbull, *A Bigger Picture*, Hardie Grant Books, 2020, p. 636.

Human Rights Commission's Respect@Work report ... the government's plan falls significantly short ... Australian Human Rights Commission, *Respect@Work: Sexual Harassment National Inquiry Report*, AHRC, 2020, humanrights.gov.au/our-work/sex-discrimination/publications/respectwork-sexual-harassment-national-inquiry-report-2020; Emma Golledge, Dianne Anagnos, Madeleine Causbrook & Sean Bowes, 'The government's "roadmap" for dealing with sexual harassment falls short. What we need is radical change', The Conversation, 8 April 2021, theconversation.com/the-governments-roadmap-for-dealing-with-sexual-harassment-falls-short-what-we-need-is-radical-change-158431

'This new eruption of power ...' Annabel Crabb, 'A new power has risen in Australian politics – and it's not coming quietly', ABC News, 28 March 2021, abc.net.au/news/2021-03-28/new-power-emerges-in-australian-politics-not-coming-quietly/100030876

'sexist backwater', 'the most unsafe workplace' Damian Cave, '"The most unsafe workplace"? Parliament, Australian women say', *The New York Times*, 5 April 2021, nytimes.com/2021/04/05/world/australia/parliament-women-rape-metoo.html

'debate of our time', 'no right answer' *A Podcast of One's Own with Julia Gillard*, Acast, 15 July 2019, play.acast.com/s/a-podcast-of-ones-own/tanyaplibersekonwomeninpolitics

'How good does it feel ...' Leigh Sales, *7.30*, ABC TV, 11 March 2021, abc.net.au/7.30/treasurer-josh-frydenberg-speaks-to-7.30/13240266

'other houses that need to be fixed up' Scott Morrison, press conference, 23 March 2021, pm.gov.au/mediapress-conference-australian-parliament-house-act-37

one in three people had experienced sexual harassment ... Australian Human Rights Commission, *Everyone's Business: Fourth National Survey on Sexual Harassment in Australian Workplaces*, 12 September 2018, humanrights.gov.au/our-work/sex-discrimination/publications/everyones-business-fourth-national-survey-sexual

61 per cent of woman and 12 per cent of men ... Review of Sexual Harassment in Victorian Courts *Preventing and Addressing Sexual Harassment in Victorian Courts: Report and Recommendations*, March 2021, shreview.courts.vic.gov.au/wp-content/uploads/2021/04/Report-and-Recommendations-Preventing-and-Addressing-Sexual-Harassment-in-Vic-Courts.pdf

'with the same level of urgency ...' Nassim Khadem, 'Corporate leaders call for end to non-disclosure agreements silencing victims of workplace sexual harassment', ABC News, 10 September 2020, abc.net.au/news/2020-09-10/companies-urged-to-change-approach-workplace-sexual-harrassment/12646874

they released a report calling for ... Champions of Change Coalition, *Disrupting the System: Preventing and Responding to Sexual Harassment in the Workplace*, 2020, championsofchangecoalition.org/wp-content/uploads/2020/09/Disrupting-the-System_Preventing-and-responding-to-sexual-harassment-in-the-workplace_CCI_web-FINAL.pdf

revised Ministerial Standards ... Australian Government, *Statement of Ministerial Standards*, 21 February 2018, apo.org.au/sites/default/files/resource-files/2018-02/apo-nid133661.pdf

'gross overreach', 'morality police' *Q+A*, ABC TV, 15 February 2018, abc.net.au/qanda/qa-metoo-special/10649600

Australian Football League sacked two executives ... Patrick Durkin, 'AFL axe falls after sex scandals', *Australian Financial Review*, 14 July 2017, afr.com/companies/sport/afl-axe-falls-after-sex-scandals-20170714-gxb9kl

'The key driver of sexual harassment is power ...' Kate Jenkins, 'Sexual harassment is prevalent across all industries and sectors. We can and must stop it', *Guardian*, 1 July 2020, theguardian.com/commentisfree/2020/jul/01/sexual-harassment-is-prevalent-across-all-industries-and-sectors-we-can-and-must-stop-it

'It is absolutely no coincidence ...' Kate Jenkins, *RN Breakfast*, ABC Radio National, 23 June 2020, abc.net.au/radionational/programs/breakfast/sex-discrimination-commissioner-on-allegations-in/12383054

'It's actually really difficult to be the only woman ...' Helen Livesy, 'What was said at the AMP staff meeting', *Australian Financial Review*, 2 July 2020, afr.com/companies/financial-services/what-was-said-at-the-amp-staff-meeting-20200702-p558dt

women are more inclined to speak to other women leaders ... Australian Human Rights Commission, *Respect@Work: Sexual Harassment National Inquiry Report*, 2020, humanrights.gov.au/our-work/sex-discrimination/publications/respectwork-sexual-harassment-national-inquiry-report-2020

'Their accounts of their experiences at the time have been believed' *Statement by the Hon Susan Kiefel AC, Chief Justice of the High Court Of Australia*, High Court of Australia, 22 June 2020, cdn.hcourt.gov.au/assets/news/Statement-by-Chief-Justice-Susan-Kiefel-AC.pdf

CHAPTER 9: In leaders we trust

'workplace coercive control', 'an abusive strategy ...' Lisa Aronson Fontes, 'Workplace coercive control" more than a "bad boss"',

Psychology Today, 11 August 2019, psychologytoday.com/au/blog/invisible-chains/201908/workplace-coercive-control-more-bad-boss

'The credit belongs to the man ...' Theodore Roosevelt, 'Citizenship in a republic', Paris, 23 April 1910.

'championed women's equality and invested ...' Anne Summers, 'Nothing will change for women while Morrison is PM', *Australian Financial Review*, 19 May 2021, afr.com/politics/federal/nothing-will-change-for-women-while-morrison-is-pm-20210318-p57c0d

'a form of madness' Malcolm Turnbull, press conference, 23 August 2018, malcolmturnbull.com.au/media/press-conference-parliament-house-canberra-23-august-2018

flashback in March 2021 when he said ... Scott Morrison, press conference, 1 March 2021; Julia Banks, 'Parliament House is the biggest boys' club in the country. It's up to Scott Morrison to change that', *Guardian*, 27 March 2021, theguardian.com/commentisfree/2021/mar/27/parliament-house-is-the-biggest-boys-club-in-the-country-its-up-to-scott-morrison-to-change-that

'Turnbull's puppet', 'revenge', 'invisible hand' Andrew Bolt, 'The revenge of Turnbull's puppet', *Herald Sun*, 5 February 2019, heraldsun.com.au/blogs/andrew-bolt/the-revenge-of-turnbulls-puppet/news-story/851a30d7f9e8a617b9334628dfcf7747; Renee Viellaris, 'Julia Banks: a puppet hellbent on revenge over Turnbull ousting', *Courier Mail*, 3 February 2019, couriermail.com.au/news/opinion/julia-banks-a-puppet-hellbent-on-revenge-over-turnbull-ousting/news-story/92c75babab94539d33005b90185aa9da; Dennis Shanahan, 'Coalition angst as Turnbull plays invisible hand', *Australian*, 29 November 2018, theaustralian.com.au/nation/politics/coalition-angst-as-turnbull-plays-invisible-hand/news-story/51231950ff5f87180803691 37bcb8d0a

'What is important right now ...' Scott Morrison, doorstop interview, 29 August 2018, pm.gov.au/media/doorstop-interview-sydney-0

My speech about refugees ... Julia Banks, Australian House of Representatives, House Hansard, 25 October 2018, pp. 11220–21.

'Often when good women call out ...' Julia Banks, Australian House of Representatives, House Hansard, 27 November 2018, p. 11571.

'We want to see women rise ...' Scott Morrison, International Women's Day Breakfast, 8 March 2019, pm.gov.au/media/remarks-international-womens-day-women-resources-breakfast

'She. Can. Go.' Scott Morrison, Australian House of Representatives, House Hansard, 22 October 2020, p. 7985.

'I think it is one of the worst acts of bullying I've ever witnessed.' Christine Holgate, *7.30*, ABC TV, 13 April 2021, abc.net.au/7.30/christine-holgate-speaks-exclusively-to-7.30/13301254

a cartoon appeared ... Matt Golding, in Jacqueline Maley, 'The Liberals' woman problem. Newsflash: it's not women who are the problem', *Sydney Morning Herald*, 27 November 2018, smh.com.au/politics/federal/coalition-liberals-woman-problem-julia-banks-20181127-p50iq1.html

CHAPTER 10: Looking in the mirror

'If he [Tony Abbott] wants to know ...' Julia Gillard, Australian House of Representatives, House Hansard, 9 October 2012, p. 11581.

'emotional start', 'it took on a life of its own' Gabrielle Chan, 'Julia Gillard explains "misogyny speech"', *Guardian*, 30 September 2013, theguardian.com/world/2013/sep/30/julia-gillard-explains-misogyny-speech

'a lower threshold for what constitutes offensive behaviour' Karina Schumann & Michael Ross, 'Why women apologize more than men: gender differences in thresholds for perceiving offensive behavior', *Psychological Science*, vol. 21, no. 11, November 2010, pp. 1649–55, p. 1651.

'bristled', 'granted she is good ...' Gail Kelly, *Live Lead Learn: My Stories of Life and Leadership*, Penguin, 2017, p. 209.

women ask for pay rises as much as men ... Ruth Whippman, 'Enough leaning in. Let's tell men to lean out', *New York Times*, 10 October 2019, nytimes.com/2019/10/10/opinion/sunday/feminism-lean-in.html

female-led countries have fared better under COVID-19. Jon Henley, 'Female-led countries handled coronavirus better, study suggests', *Guardian*, 18 August 2020, theguardian.com/world/2020/aug/18/female-led-countries-handled-coronavirus-better-study-jacinda-ardern-angela-merkel

'I'm very proudly an empathetic, compassionately driven politician ...' 'Jacinda Ardern: "It Takes Strength to Be an Empathetic Leader"', BBC News, 14 November 2018, bbc.com/news/av/world-asia-46207254

'You can be strong, and you can be kind.' Jacinda Ardern, *Today Show*, NBC, 24 September 2018, today.com/video/new-zealand-s-prime-minister-talks-about-being-a-new-mom-and-world-leader-1327697475816

'There are people who practice being authentic ...' Brené Brown, *The Gifts of Imperfection: Let Go of Who You Think You're Supposed to Be and Embrace Who You Are*, Hazelden, 2010, p. 67.

'To those who say politics is not for the faint hearted ...' Julia Banks, Australian House of Representatives, House Hansard, 27 November 2018, p. 11571.

'Can I just add to that ...' Josh Frydenberg and Scott Morrison, press conference, 27 November 2018, pm.gov.au/media/press-conference-treasurer

'Having been married for forty-five years ...' Ted Yoho, United States of America, *Congressional Record: House of Representatives*, vol. 166, no. 129, 22 July 2020, p. H6321, congress.gov/116/crec/2020/07/22/CREC-2020-07-22-pt1-PgH3621.pdf

'What I do have issue with …' Alexandria Ocasio-Cortez, United States of America, *Congressional Record: House of Representatives*, vol. 166, no. 130, 23 July 2020, p. H3703, congress.gov/116/crec/2020/07/23/CREC-2020-07-23-pt1-PgH3702-2.pdf

'a way of clarifying things', 'as a father' Scott Morrison, doorstop interview, 16 February 2021, pm.gov.au/media/doorstop-interview-australian-parliament-house-act-160221

'it shouldn't take having children to have a conscience …' Grace Tame, responding to question by Naveen Razik, following address to National Press Club, *Guardian*, 3 March 2021, youtu.be/dMxcSJ8ZlBE

'The eloquent, audacious, courageous statement of disruption …' Nikki Gemmell (@NikkiGemmell), 27 November 2018, twitter.com/NikkiGemmell/status/1067251848459968513

Acknowledgements

My thanks to everyone who said, 'You should write a book.'

To Sandy Grant and the team at Hardie Grant, especially to Emily Hart, for her wisdom, intellect and kindness.

To the wonderful people from all walks of life who I wouldn't otherwise have met if not for my legal, corporate and political career, and with whom I know I shall have enduring friendships.

To all my friends, old and new, for their love and support, and with a special thanks to my women friends, who always have a special place in my heart.

To my late father, my mother and my brother for planting the seed of family love in my life.

And to my husband, and our son and daughter. Their support is what harnesses the personal power in me to continue to do what I do, and they fill my heart with love every single day.